A LATE EDUCATION

IN THE DESERT
Alex Clifford (*right*) and Alan Moorehead

ALAN MOOREHEAD

A Late Education

Episodes in a Life

HAMISH HAMILTON

LONDON

*First published in Great Britain
by Hamish Hamilton Ltd 1970
90 Great Russell Street London W.C.1*

SBN 241 01986 9

P15
M65
A3

To
Martha and Laura

92
M82 15

*Printed in Great Britain
by Ebenezer Baylis and Son Ltd.
The Trinity Press, Worcester, and London*

CONTENTS

To the Edgware Road I

ANYONE who was involved in the Spanish Civil
War on the Franco side will remember St Jean de
Luz on the Basque coast in southern France. Like
the town of Riga in the Russian revolution it was a
neutral staging-post on the edge of the conflict, and every
traveller, whether he was a black-marketeer, a diplomat,
a secret agent or a journalist would pause there for a while
on his journeys in and out of Spain.

In St Jean de Luz you could get anything from a forged
passport to a million-peseta small-arms contract, and it
was a remarkable place for intrigue. Had the French
government not kept order there would have been serious
disturbances in the town, since the foreign colony and
many of the French themselves were sharply divided into
two camps—those who were for Franco and those who
were against him—and they hated one another with a
deep emotional hatred.

The centre of all this agitation was a cheerful little
restaurant called the Bar Basque that still exists in the
main street, and sooner or later everyone of any con-
sequence made their way there in order to read the
newspapers and pick up the latest gossip. There was no
item of news about the fighting, whether it was the ship-
ment of tanks from Russia or Moors from Morocco, the
destruction of Guernica or the rising of the Fifth Column
in Madrid, that was not either invented in the Bar Basque
or discussed there with embellishments early in its course
round the town.

Outwardly there was nothing sinister about the Bar
Basque: you might have taken it as just another fashionable

seaside restaurant that possibly merited a star in the Michelin guidebook. There were Basque murals on the walls, scenes of pelota players and peasants dancing the *jota*, and the decor was rustic walnut and red plush, all of it very comfortable and modern. People took their aperitifs under striped umbrellas in the street, where a line of horse-drawn cabs stood waiting under the trees, and then towards one in the afternoon and eight or nine in the evening the restaurant began to fill. One ate *jambon de Bayonne* (which was said to have lain all winter, salted and raw, maturing under the snow of the Pyrenees), *langoustines*, anchovies and tiny eels, *angouilles*, that were brought in each morning by fishing boats from the Atlantic, red and green pepper salads, jam omelettes and melons. On Thursday nights there was a cabaret and a dance, and they served a dish of roast duck cooked with peaches, oranges and green peas. The wine was the local rosé or Bordeaux, brought from the vineyards on the Garonne only three or four hours away by road, and after the meal one drank a local liqueur, pale and sticky, called *Fleurs d'Hendaye*.

I remember these lucullan details so well because it was at the Bar Basque that I first met Alex in 1938, and in the years that followed the roast duck, the dancing of the *jota* and the wine became for us symbols of the good lost life to which we hoped to return one day. Through the lean nineteen-forties we thought of the place almost as nostalgically as an ageing woman will recall some romantic moment in her past, a ball, an evening at the theatre, a holiday by the sea, when she first fell in love.

There was, however, nothing very satisfactory about this first meeting; indeed, it was a disaster. I had come down from Paris on the overnight train and had made my way directly from the station to the Bar Basque, hoping that I might find there some acquaintance who would give me the news and help me find my way about the town. I was a little diffident about going inside, partly because I spoke bad French and partly because places like this were rather outside my range. Otto, the barman, was however immediately helpful. He nodded towards one of the red plush banquettes against the wall where two men were sitting. One of them, he said—the one with glasses—was Alexander Clifford, the Reuters correspondent, the other Karl Robson of the London *Daily Telegraph*. Robson had an air of extreme gentleness and he was astonishingly handsome, an El Greco figure, thin, mild and suffering. Clifford's appearance, on the other hand, was rather forbidding: a round head, a broad cerebral brow and a tight-looking mouth. He peered in an uncompromising way through his glasses. Yet for some reason I went to him first and introduced myself. He muttered something in reply and went on with his dinner. I asked then if he knew of any place where I could stay, and he looked up at me with an air of polite irritation, obviously resenting the interruption and wanting to go on with his conversation with Robson. This surely, when one is young, is the worst of trials, to be snubbed by a stranger in a public place. I stood there waiting and it was Robson who spoke at last. 'I should try the Golf Hotel,' he said and I retreated to the bar too confused to do anything but take my bags and go.

It was not until April 1940 that I saw Alex again, and by then things had greatly changed. The Second World War had broken out, and two years' experience as a newspaper correspondent, at first in France and then in Italy, had given me a little more confidence in dealing with foreign languages and places. I had had an uneasy time among the Fascists in Italy, never knowing from week to week whether or not Mussolini was going to come into the war on the German side, and now that it seemed certain that he would do so I had flown across to neutral Greece to await events. At the Grande Bretagne Hotel in Athens I learned that a friend of mine, a man named Morell, was

1*

lying ill in bed, and I went up to see him. There was only one other passenger in the lift and I was aware of a certain familiarity in the large, almost Prussian head, the heavy shoulders and the air of superiority and pernickety indifference; and I remembered then that this was Alexander Clifford and that I disliked him very much. He was not quite so imposing as he had appeared to be in the Bar Basque in 1938, but he was still not a companion I would have chosen, even in a lift. When we got out at the same floor it was embarrassingly apparent that he too was visiting Morell, and so there was nothing for it but that we should knock at the door and go into the sick room together. Sitting at the bedside we were careful to address our remarks to Morell, never to one another, and it was an uneasy and fruitless conversation. I was about to get up and go, explaining that I would return later in the day, when the doctor arrived. This made it necessary for Alex and me to leave together.

Once again we paced along the corridor in silence and waited for the lift. But it was ridiculous to continue like this, and for the sake of something to say I suggested that we should have a drink. To my surprise Alex agreed at once, and we found a taverna round the corner from the hotel. He thought that ouzo, the Greek pernod, was the drink to take at that hour, and ordered it from the waiter in Greek. Had he remembered our first meeting in St Jean de Luz, I asked. Yes, he answered, he believed he did. He added water from the carafe to his ouzo and watched it turn smoky white in the glass, waiting for me to go on. Was he still with Reuters, I asked. No, he said, he had been with Reuters on the Western front but now he had joined the staff of the London *Daily Mail* and was on a vague general assignment in the Balkans. He said this defensively and reluctantly, as though it were something of which he was half ashamed, and he kept looking away from me towards the traffic in the street. Suddenly I began to see that he was shy; not only shy in relationship to me but genuinely uncertain of all his affairs, and particularly of the reasons that had brought him here to Athens at this moment when it was so far away from England and the war.

He was filled with gloom about the war. He thought the Germans were better soldiers than ours and the Nazis had a better army. I listened to this subversive talk in astonishment, and then answered him with the stock war-time propaganda, which seemed so definite and irrefutable in the spring of 1940: the Allies had the oil, the money and the manpower. I myself, I said, had just arrived from Italy, and even if Italy came in on the German side then it would make no difference, for the Fascists were half-hearted, venal and frightened. In Germany the enemy were already short of food.

'They're not,' he said.

We argued then for three hours or more, sitting at the rickety wooden table, drinking ouzo, turning away the boot-blacks, the sellers of pistachio nuts and lottery tickets, and watching the evening transformation of Athens when the dust and the heat subside at last and for half an hour the air achieves the clear and buoyant colour of a rock pool in the tropics. The bright lamp of the moon came up over Hymettus as we went on talking.

All this happened more than thirty years ago, and I cannot remember now just how the change from cold to warmth came over our feelings, but we must have grown very intimate before the end of the evening since we agreed to continue our travels together from that point onwards. Young journalists thought very much about their careers at that time. Should they enlist? Or was their work a sufficient excuse for them to continue in their jobs as most of them in their hearts wanted to do? Alex was fairly definite about this. The thing to do, he said, was to become a war correspondent. A British military headquarters was already established in Cairo, and if Italy came into the war a new front was bound to open up in the Middle East. But how to get our newspapers to send us there? I was still a very junior member of the foreign staff of the *Daily Express*, Alex had joined the *Mail* only a few weeks before, and neither of us were in any position to dictate our movements to our editors. There was a good deal of rivalry between the *Express* and the *Mail*, and in the end we decided to use this to our own advantage. Alex would wire his paper: 'Moorehead of the *Express* proceeding to Cairo stop shall I follow?' while I warned my people that Clifford of the *Mail* was setting off in the same direction. The implications of course in both messages was that we were possessed of mysterious and important information which we could not divulge in a telegram because of wartime censorship. It was not quite such a dishonest proceeding as it might appear to be, for we really did believe we would be more useful in Egypt than in Greece. To involve ourselves in the war seemed, at that moment, to be the only worthwhile aim in life, and surely, we argued, we would be better reporters than soldiers.

Automatically the telegrams from London came back: 'Follow Clifford,' 'Follow Moorehead,' and Alex and I booked our passages to Cairo.

It was a pleasant flight. The British airline was still using flying-boats in those days, and they were more solid and comfortable than any flying machine that has since been invented. I remember our coming down at Suda Bay in Crete, and when the steward opened the oval-shaped door we gazed down into sparkling water that had the same colour and transparency as the sky. The sunshine made converging shafts of silver-yellow light down into the deep, and shoals of little fishes came darting past the aluminium hull of the flying-boat. There were only one or two other passengers. We took off our clothes and dived straight into the water from the open doorway.

In Egypt the early summer heat was beginning, and it was less tolerable than it became later on, because we were not used to it and our clothes were too heavy. I knew Cairo a little from a previous trip, and led the way to the Carlton Hotel, which was cheaper than Shepheards or the Continental-Savoy; we had shower-closets instead of bathrooms, and nearly all night long, in the Egyptian café below, the clients banged down their dominoes and backgammon pieces with a noise that had the same power to destroy sleep as a creaking door. An open air cinema stood opposite, and until midnight the arabic dialogue, the incidental music and the pistol shots of the westerns came up to us in a loud, meaningless explosion of sound. But these were merely incidental discomforts, and we were much too busy to care about them.

We had arrived at a crucial moment; preparations were being made to establish a new front in the western desert of Egypt, and war correspondents were being enrolled at the British headquarters in Cairo. We spent an intriguing day getting our kit from the Officers' Shop at the Kasr-el-Nil barracks in Cairo. We bought desert boots made of suede that came half way up the ankle, knee-length khaki stockings, shorts of khaki drill that fastened with two neat buckles at the midriff, drill shirts, and the whole was surmounted by the regulation khaki sun helmet. (It was not until a year or two later that the Army at last agreed that sunstroke came through the eyes and not through the back of the neck, and thereafter we wore peaked caps or berets.) We were given, also, water bottles, gas masks, flat steel helmets and, for the first and only time in the war, a revolver each. The revolver, we were told, was not to be used against the enemy but against the local population in case it turned against us. Finally we bought mosquito nets, camp beds, sleeping bags and canvas washing buckets; and we were complete. There was as yet, however, no war in the Middle East.

April slipped by very agreeably. Most of our meals were eaten at the Gezira Sporting Club, on an island in the Nile, where a buffet lunch of some pretensions was served. The menu included, I remember, delicious little cold mutton chops, and we discovered a Palestinian white wine which was bottled in Italian fiaschi and cost 20 piastres, or four English shillings. We bought silk from the looms in the bazaar, we joined the Turf Club, we visited the Great Pyramid (which Alex climbed—a thing impossible for me because of vertigo), and we watched Egyptian dancers at the nightclubs on the Nile.

Through the day we busied ourselves with collecting what scraps of information we could and cabling them off to our newspapers. We bought large-scale maps of the desert, we debated strategy and the confused politics of the Middle East, and we made friends with the other journalists and some of the officers at headquarters. Alex at least had had a few months on the static western front in France, but I knew nothing of the army and still less of the air force and the navy. To me it was all new, exciting and potentially dangerous. I disliked the little green tabs we were obliged to wear on our shoulders. They were inscribed in gold 'British War Correspondent' and gave one the feeling of being a delegate at a Rotary convention. War correspondents were rare birds at that time, and people in the Turf Club were forever sidling up to us, arching their necks to read the inscription, and, having read it, they were apt to laugh facetiously among their friends. This was unpleasant, for at heart we took our-selves rather seriously and were already in imagination projecting ourselves into all sorts of heroic dangers at the front.

But there was still no front in the first week of May, and the days went apathetically by; it seemed that we might drift on like this forever. However, I began to know Alex a good deal better. I soon discovered that he was not nearly so interested in the Egyptian dancers as I was and the music made him feel slightly ill. When we went one night to hear a German-Jewish orchestra from Palestine play a programme of Beethoven and Wagner I was astonished to discover that he knew every note. Afterwards he criticized the performance in terms that were incomprehensible to me. I did not know then that music for him was something more than a dilettante pleasure— he himself played the violin and composed a little—and since I am tone deaf it remained a region of experience where we could never meet. We had another blank spot: he did not seem to be strongly drawn towards women in a physical way, and apparently could exist quite happily without them, which I could not. He was certainly not homosexual, and enjoyed being with women, but he never appeared to feel the desire to touch them or caress them; this was reserved for small babies and cats. He could never resist taking a cat on his knee, and often I would find him among the babies that were still being perambulated by English nursemaids through the green lawns of Gezira.

He seemed to me to be rather mean over money. If someone ordered a round of drinks it was not Alex. I kept our communal accounts because I was the one who usually had the cash ready, and Alex criticized my book-keeping rather sharply at times. He pointed out that he *never* smoked, and if I liked to provide cigarettes for our guests then that was my affair. He was almost a vegetarian, and since I ate the expensive meat dishes he was careful not to pay for more than his share when we dined in a restaurant. At first I could not understand this caution; financially we were both doing very well. Neither of us had any money in the bank, but we each had from our newspapers two guineas a day for expenses, my salary was £12 a week and Alex's somewhat more. It may even have been £20 a week. Moreover, he was a bachelor and I had been married six months before.

He had another trait which was upsetting at times. Stupidity was apt to send him into a sudden quiet rage. He barked at officials, often he seemed arrogant and over-bearing, and I found myself constantly trying to smooth down the feelings of some ruffled lieutenant of intelligence or official to whom he had been rude. Just at that moment it seemed to me to be foolish to make enemies of these people.

These outbursts of Alex's were the more remarkable because he was often so weak and indecisive in other ways. When we visited some brass hat in his office I was the one who had to go first and knock at the door. I asked the awkward question and made all the arrangements about where we should go, whom we should meet and how we should handle the dispatches we were sending home to our papers. Alex liked me to make a proposal and then he would feel free to criticize. Often I irritated him. He simply could not understand the mentality of anyone who could not spell, who was inaccurate about times and places and who could never remember names; to him all this was either affectation or pure laziness, and in any case a bore. My ignorance he was prepared to put up with, since I had been born in Australia which he regarded as semi-barbaric. But he found most of my ideas, my 'genera-lizations' as he called them, to be wild, reckless guesswork and nearly always wrong. Moreover, we approached every event in our lives from precisely opposite standpoints. Alex was immediately sure that things would go wrong, I was equally certain that they would not, and if they did then some new factor I thought would emerge to put them right again.

He had a morbid notion that he would die in the Edgware Road. I do not know why he should have fixed on that very ordinary shopping street in London (though it was a good deal shabbier than it is today), but it represented for him a way of life which he instinctively feared and loathed.

Perhaps he felt that the Edgware Road, the world of small suburban cafés, was his true provenance, and unless he was very careful it would rise up one day and reclaim him.

I too had my Edgware Road in Australia where I had been born, and had devoted a good deal of energy to escaping from it. I did not fear or hate Australia, but by this time I did not feel that I really belonged to it; I had made my home in Europe. When I remembered the early part of my life—the first twenty-five years of which had been spent in Australia—it was not altogether with the sentimental glow which the exile is supposed to feel about his birthplace.

For God, Country and Letters

God knows I was never maltreated as a child; I was loved, and as the third child probably spoiled as well, and there had certainly been no horrendous, Dickensian background of wicked schoolmasters or unhappy family life. My school in Melbourne, Scotch College, was one of the best in the country, and yet later when I thought about it I found myself oppressed by sensations of frustration and despair.

I had been a most unsuccessful schoolboy, invariably at the bottom of my class and unable to get into any of the teams, but this hardly explains the sense of loathing—yes, positively loathing—that still overcomes me whenever I think of that place. I attended the school as a day-boy for ten years, and surely there must have been pleasant episodes in all that time. Yet all I can remember now is those meaningless morning prayers, the heat of those over-crowded classrooms through the long droning afternoon, those second-rate masters brought out from England with their harassed and defeated faces, those windy red-brick corridors with their clanging metal shutters, and the dead hand of suburbia over all. The bearded dominie who was the headmaster was, I believe, a kindly man and much loved, but to me he was an ogre and I still have a feeling of panic when I recall that awful voice, 'You boy. Come here.'

Clearly all this is very unfair, and indeed my sister, who is some years older than I am, has told me that I was a cheerful and happy little boy, and although I did not do very well at my lessons I was as bright as a button.

But I see a different picture. I see a small boy walking home in the late afternoon, and he has on his head a faded cloth cap with alternating stripes of cardinal, gold and blue radiating downward from a button at the top. The school badge attached to the front of this cap is an oval medallion, silver in colour, and it displays a seated, toga-clad figure whom I take to be some sort of a Greek god, probably the god of learning; he is reading a tablet and an oil lamp burns on a pedestal at his side; around this figure is the school motto: *Deo Patriae Litteris*. It is not a bad sort of badge, and I remember feeling disappointed a year or two later when they replaced the classical figure—was he too pagan?—by the burning bush of Moses. My sweater is red with gold and blue bands around the wrists and throat, the laces of my boots are criss-crossed between little metal stubs, and the leather satchel strapped to my shoulders contains my wooden pencil case and my hateful books. Nothing is new. My sweater is darned and so are my socks that are held up by black elastic garters. My boots need mending. The cardboard that supports the peak of my cap is broken and is beginning to show through the cloth, and that is because I have so many times rolled up the cap and shoved it into my trouser pockets or have used it to beat my companions when we have been playing or fighting.

Just now I am alone, and I am late getting back from school because I have once again been kept in for an extra hour as a punishment for doing my homework badly. I know that I will do my homework badly again tonight, and that I will be kept in again tomorrow, and that at the end of the term I will be, as usual, the boy with the lowest marks. I am not particularly lazy or defiant of authority; I simply cannot understand what the masters are saying or the symbols chalked on the blackboard or the words printed in the books. I do not like being at the bottom of the class. I hate it. It fills me with shame and resentment. There are other stupid boys in the class but somehow they manage to get by and most of them are bigger and faster on their feet than I am, and they find a place in the cricket teams in summer and the football team in winter—a thing I can never hope to do. And so I am a withdrawn and rather sullen little boy and I can see no hope of escape; the avenging master stands over me and the monotonous treadmill will go on and on forever.

Where is the truth? If my sister is right then I must have been a mighty self-pitier and self-deceiver. Either that, or I must have learned, even at that early age, the value of setting up a façade between myself and the world, an outward show of confidence that was designed, as a form of self-protection, to mask my weakness and un-certainty. Does a small boy ever really tell you what is going on in his inmost mind? Does he know himself? Per-haps at that stage I was unteachable and the school could never have helped me. It is hard to say. But whatever may be the truth of the matter I know that my memory of that long incarceration still persists and it is a memory that I wish I could forget.

Nor was my spiritual life in much better case. We all had to go to Sunday School when we were very young, and later on it was church every Sunday morning. Can there have been anything in the world so dreary as those Presbyterian services of the nineteen-twenties, anything so calculated to alienate a child from religion? The hard seats, the arid and interminable sermons, the thin, flat singing of the hymns, the woe-begone and accusing images in cheap stained glass and mass-produced plaster—it was all one long punishment, and my only moment of inspiration came when the doors were opened and I sighted sweet freedom in the sunshine outside. Then with a full heart I could give praise to God. My dislike of the church was such that it even survived a short period, just prior to my leaving school, when I was extremely devout, pouring out my prayers each night on bended knees, carrying my pocket-bible with me everywhere, pausing to close my eyes a dozen—twenty—times a day to ask a blessing. Even at the height of this fervour I would never willingly go to church; indeed, I resented the church even more because I felt that the utter dullness of the service would be an insult to my shining God.

But then there were the holidays. Here the picture is much brighter. I see the small boy now riding in a coach drawn by four sweating horses. We climb steadily up into the hills through the streaming rain, with the tree-ferns and the blue gums on either side, and I can feel the black leather seat under my behind, and see the steam rising from the horses' backs, and smell the fresh turds they let fall as they lift their tails. On we go, hour after hour, bumping and lurching on the muddy track, and it is a mixture of weariness and bliss. I am off with my family into the hills for the autumn holidays. There will be hot scones, strawberry jam and clotted cream for tea and a steak with an egg on top for breakfast. I will fish in the creek, I will see the mighty chips fly when the handyman fells a tree, and I will go down into a wet fern-filled gully, and with luck will hear a lyre-bird imitating all the sounds of the bush—even the *clonk clonk* of the handyman's axe. At night there will be great eucalyptus logs burning in the open fireplace, and my mother will accompany us while we sing *Tramp, Tramp, Tramp the Boys are Marching*, and *It's a Long Way to Tipperary*, and *Pack Up Your Troubles in Your Old Kit Bag*, and *There's a Long Long Trail a-Winding*, and selections from Gilbert and Sullivan, and the one about Antonio we all love:

Oh, Oh, Antonio, he's gone away
Left me alone-io
All on my own-io.
I want to meet him
With his new sweet-heart,
Then up will go Antonio
And his ice-cream cart.

The room is lit by a big glass lamp with a canvas wick, like a rat's tail, floating in the kerosene, and when we go to bed we will take our candles with us, and safe between the sheets we will hear a dingo howling somewhere in the distance.

Then again in the long hot summer we are camping under the ti-trees on a beach that stretches away as far as the eye can see and not another human being in sight. I cringe a little at the first shock of the half-cold sea in the early morning, but then slowly, gently and inevitably a curling breaker has picked me up, is racing me back to the shore, is depositing me high and dry on the yellow sand. Then back again for more. In the rock pools little cat-fish dart about through strands of waving kelp, and I can see the salt caking white on my arms under the hot sun as I walk back along the beach to breakfast. Someone has put a green twig over the billy of tea to stop it tasting of smoke and the chops are spitting into the red eye of the open fire.

And again I am riding across the great bare plains of the Riverina behind a mob of sheep, and it is marvellous to watch the kangaroos bounding away as we approach. It is not so much hopping as a forward-flowing movement, something between bounding and running. Their fat tails hit the ground with a decided thump and every so often they come to a stop on their haunches and look back at you with an air of gentle enquiry and then go on again. A flock of pink and grey cockatoos breaks away from a dead gum-tree, a wedge-tailed eagle spirals slowly upwards into the pale blue sky, and in the distance a twisted sheet of galvanized iron, the only incident that interrupts the eye on the way to the horizon, will glow red in the morning with the first red rays of the sun. All the soil is red as well, blood-red at that early hour.

The bush was an escape from imitation. The school, the church, the city itself were all copies of older institutions in England. But the bush imitated nothing, it was *sui generis*, the best that could be. And it was still at our door-steps in the nineteen-twenties. Half an hour's train journey from Melbourne took you to townships where there were no made roads, where people got about on horseback or in two-wheeled buggies, and in the surrounding scrub it was still possible to get a glimpse of a wallaby or of a wombat which is a black coarse-haired burrowing bear. The great onslaught upon the bush was only just beginning—the cutting down and ring-barking of the eucalyptus forests to make way for grazing land—and no one then could have envisaged a time when so much of this countryside would become tamed and urbanized and even uglier than the American middle west. We thought the bush, like the British Empire, was there forever; it was so old and there was so much of it.

Things began to go a little better at school as I got on a bit. I made a friend or two, I was given the job of coxswain to the third crew, and the work seemed a little less incomprehensible in the higher grades where one was allowed a choice of subjects. With the help of an indulgent examiner I just managed to matriculate. But I was still a very long way from living up to the school motto. God, or at any rate the Presbyterian God, was like the headmaster, an avenger; Country (in the sense of patriotism) I had not yet much thought about, and Learning, although I yearned for it, was still an inexplicable maze.

The school fees in those days were not very high, but even so I do not know how my father managed to pay them for he was a journalist, and journalists in Australia then were badly paid. We were the genteel poor and in a country with so few inhabitants that was almost the worst sort of poor to be; we could never hide. However much we affected to be above trade and the working class the butcher was bound to appear at the door and make a scene about his unpaid bill, and the neighbours were bound to know about it. All the things that would have made life easy for us we could not do; we had to live in a respectable, non-working class district, keep a maid and travel first class in the trains. I say 'we', because we children approved of my parents' attitude in this matter; we were not the working class and that was that, and because of my father's literary connections I even grew to consider myself superior to my more well-to-do relatives, most of whom were engaged in trade. But it was a humiliating struggle to keep up appearances. I rubbed in ink to hide the darn in my blue trousers. I patched up the broken strings of my tennis racquet for the thousandth time. I pretended that I did not want to go to the movies whereas the true reason was that I could not afford the price of the ticket.

My parents were forever moving. I suppose during my schooldays we must have lived in almost a dozen different flats and houses in the suburbs of Melbourne, and heaven knows what effort these upheavals must have required, especially from my mother. At the time there always seemed to be some valid reason for making a change—the new place had a better garden, or was cheaper, or was nearer to the tram—and for us children it was always tremendous fun; I loved setting myself up in a new bedroom with a new view and helping to tack up the curtains and the pictures. Life began again. But looking back on it now I think there was great distress behind this restlessness. Somewhere, somehow, my parents must have felt, there was a better life to be had, an escape from the squalid pettiness of counting every penny, and if you moved on perhaps *something* would happen to turn the tide. At all events you got credit with the tradesmen when you first arrived at a new house and the butcher was polite. And once again in all this I think we children supported our parents. We were really very fond of them and that Micawberish and futile optimism became infectious. Our well-to-do uncles and aunts who stayed securely in the same place seemed much less amusing.

It was somewhere about this period of which I am writing, probably at the age of fifteen, not long before I left school, that I decided that I was going to become a writer, and I even fixed on the means by which this was going to be achieved. I would start, I decided, on one of the Australian newspapers and then I would go abroad and somehow get a job as a foreign correspondent. After that my real career would begin: the writing of books.

Obviously it was the fact that my father was a journalist that first involved me in the idea of writing. Perhaps too, a genetic spiral descended from my maternal grandfather whom I never saw but who was much involved in print. He seems to have been an energetic and resourceful man and I wish I could have known him. Migrating to Australia from England towards the middle of last century he rose from foreman to be the owner of a flourishing printing business which enabled him to live in a large house and to drive his own coach and pair. In the course of his short life—he died in his fifties—he taught himself several languages and wrote a book or two. I never did succeed in finding out what became of his money when he died. All I know is that by the time I left school there was no question of my going on to the university, which was the object upon which I had set my heart; I had to start earning money at once. A job was found for me in a small advertising agency, and between running errands as a messenger boy I learned about lay-outs, copy-writing, market-research and the whims of clients. I stuck it for six months and then presented myself to the editor of a glossy magazine named *Table Talk*. How would he like to publish a weekly column of notes from the university— news about the sports, the social clubs and all the other undergraduate activities? It was not a bad idea and he agreed to give it a trial. Payment was to be 2½d. a line, which worked out at roughly £2 10s. 0d. a week if I succeeded in filling a column. Upon this I enrolled myself at the Melbourne university, and there I remained for the next five years, paying my way at first through the *Table Talk* column, and then, rather more profitably, as the correspondent of an evening paper, the *Melbourne Herald*.

It so happened that I reached the university when it was going through a political phase. Most of the undergraduates were too young to remember much about the first world war which, in any case, had been fought thousands of miles away on the other side of the world. But there was a small group who felt strongly that something ought to be done to prevent such senseless and useless butchery from ever happening again. We were all for Karl Marx and the brotherhood of man. The Russian experiment was then only ten years old, and there was still a good deal of freshness and fervour about it, especially as we only knew of it at secondhand, and especially in a place like Australia where many of the restrictions on our lives were absurd. No pub could keep its doors open after six p.m., no newspaper could publish on Sunday, and any book, good or bad, that dealt openly with sex was instantly banned. As for the brotherhood of man, Australians had no truck with that at all—no coloured man could set foot in the country and any visiting foreigner who advocated communism was shipped back to his own country at once.

No doubt we would have challenged traditions anyway, that is what undergraduates usually do. But then in 1929 the Wall Street crash occurred and its repercussions were particularly severe in Australia, where so few people had amassed any savings to tide them through. I don't think we had any breadlines such as they had in England, but I can remember one of my well-to-do aunts sending around groceries so that my mother would be able to give us something for dinner. It was like a period of phenomenal bad weather; nobody knew what had caused it or how long it was going to last. It simply got worse and worse; and in some ways depressions are more disastrous than wars, for wars are action and generate energy, while depressions are paralysis.

I used to have long discussions with a friend called Jim Kilvington, who was somewhat different from my other companions at the university. He was a modest and charming young man, and although he was studying law he had nothing much to do with the politicians or the Labour Club. As the son of a successful surgeon he was more comfortably off than I was, and when we were studying for our exams I used to go to his home to relax in the evening. The wine was poured, the gramophone was put on, the log fire was lit in the billiard room, and we would play for an hour or two. His passion for music was such that he possessed and constantly added to an immense collection of classical and operatic records. He corresponded with other collectors and no oddity could be offered for sale or exchange—some first faint scratchy recording of Caruso's voice—but that he pounced upon it. Yet he would never, he declared, learn to play any instrument himself since he could never hope to be perfect at it. And since perfection in practically anything we did in life was impossible, the thing to do was to stand aside and be an audience. Well and good, he would become a lawyer, but he did not expect to excel at the law; he would not even try to.

This passive approach did not suit my book at all. How did he know, I demanded, that he could not become a great musician if he never even bothered to try and play the piano? Even if he ended up as merely an average musician surely that was something? Surely we had a duty to find out what was in us and do the best we could? But no, he could not be shaken; the fire of genius, he said, was not in him, and if he could not become a perfect performer then the next best thing was to be an appreciative listener.

I see now that I was drawn to Jim because he had so

many of Alex's qualities—his reluctance, his fastidious-
ness, his intelligent pessimism—and I find it unbelievable
that I should have lost touch with him and that I never
attempted to renew our friendship after I left the university. Did he lack the chic of the revolutionaries? I saw
him once again, many years later and just before he died,
when he came up to me in a bookshop in Melbourne, and
for a moment I did not recognize that rather gaunt and
kindly face. 'You remember me—Jim Kilvington?' I wish
he had not felt he had to say that. It wasn't really necessary—I would have remembered after another second—
and indeed I remember him now rather more clearly than
most of my other contemporaries at the university.
Although we talked happily and easily there was something in his manner that suggested that I had had the
better of the argument, that my pursuit of the impossible
had been worthwhile after all, whereas his own life, by
contrast, had fallen away. How much I would have dis-
agreed with him. Had we been able to bring the matter
out into the open at that short and tenuous meeting I
would have told him that I now realized that I had been
caught up in a net of fallacies: that the masterpiece I had
hoped to write was never on the cards, that the dream of
perfection should somehow have been converted into a
spiritual faith, that my conviction that I was in charge of
my own destiny and had to *make* things happen or nothing
would happen at all, was nothing more than arrogance and
a short cut to unhappiness. By moving about so much and
attempting so many different things I had rejected life
instead of discovering it, and like Baudelaire's Traveller
had ended nowhere. Well, perhaps not nowhere, but at all
events at no safer or better haven than he had reached.
How far had I advanced into the darkness? An inch more
than he had?

And then there was my brother Bernard. Far from having Jim's acceptance and detachment he found it impossible

to come to terms with the world at all. He was four years older than I was, and because he was gauche, because he seemed to fail at everything he did, and was so slow in all his reactions, I taunted him and made fun of him, deliberately provoked him, until at last he would sometimes turn on me and hit me and I would go howling to my mother. Perhaps my load of guilt makes me exaggerate, perhaps I was not quite so odious as this, but certainly I never understood him, nor did I have any real sympathy with him until one day we had a cable from Hong Kong, where he had gone to work as an architect, saying that he had died of pernicious anaemia. He was twenty-five. I remember him best sitting on the stairs of one or the other of our rented houses, playing the mouth-organ or the guitar for hour after hour until we went nearly mad at the sound, and I would come rushing in a passion from my bedroom saying that it was impossible to work and would not my parents tell him to stop at once? They stopped him. It was not until years later that I realized that he was an extremely shy and sensitive boy, and that he might have done very well at his music had anyone ever bothered to encourage him and let him take lessons. He had talent as a draughtsman too; his architectural drawings were really very good. But as things were he was pushed into one unsuitable job after another, and sooner or later he always got the sack. They said he was sullen, dull, unresponsive. Then he would hang about idly for weeks on end, and as his little store of confidence ran out he became gruff and moody, flashing out at times in sudden rages, a Caliban. He hated to get out of bed in the morning, he never could bring himself to look people in the eye, and one might have known from his sallow pimply skin and his lassitude that he was not well. Perhaps he was sent to doctors—I can't recall—perhaps something was done, but at all events it was decided to pack him off to Hong Kong. I remember that one of my aunts who was rather fond of him came to say goodbye, and she said, 'Bernie, you must look at people when they speak to you and try and smile.' He forced himself to glance at her for a moment and achieved a twisted wolfish grin. This is painful to look back upon now, but even if I had known of his early rendezvous with life's final rejection of him in Hong Kong I wonder whether I would have been kinder to him. Yes, perhaps I would have been, but only a little. To me he was simply odd, intractable, someone not to resemble, and in any case I was much too caught up with myself and my own frustrations to bother very much about his problems.

I was approaching twenty by this time, and the chief of these frustrations was concerned with sex. It appeared to be an insoluble dilemma; on the one hand one had one's fragile, reverent dream of the divine and beautiful creature whom one would not be worthy to touch, and on the other hand there was one's clamorous physical need to seduce a girl, any girl as long as she was desirable and pretty. I seemed to be spectacularly unsuccessful at this pursuit, and I put this down in great part to my being so short. I minded terribly about not being tall. At dances I constantly found myself looking *up* into my partner's face and this was mortifying. There was always the possibility, of course, of talking the girls into submission when you got them into a car outside, and how often was I carried away by my own eloquence. Surely, I felt, they must see the turbulence they had stirred up in me, my desperate wanting; how could they go on resisting? Yet they did. One got a certain distance—the wet kiss, the fumbling with the shoulder strap—and then no more.

It seems incredible that anyone could have been so ignorant about sex as I was. The only information on the subject I can remember receiving as a young boy was a dire warning: a doctor drew me aside to tell me that masturbation led to insanity and probably blindness as well if, by any chance, some of my semen was transferred to my eyes. I knew nothing, wanted to know nothing, about the workings of women's bodies, their menstrual periods and so on; all that was too embarrassing. Since I was so wholly concentrated upon my own desires I had no notion of what their emotions and physical reactions might be; I simply presumed that since I was enjoying the experience they were too, and probably in the same way. There were certain rules to be observed—one stopped a good deal short of attempting rape—but essentially it was a contest, a trial of strength, and the triumph of breaking down a girl's defences, of bringing her to an emotional pitch where she betrayed herself and could resist no more, was almost as satisfactory as the hasty and awkward consummation of the sexual act itself. And that was that. Immediately afterwards one wanted to get away as quickly as one decently could; a final perfunctory and patronizing embrace and then, 'I suppose we had better go.' Contraception one did not bother about. That was the girl's affair, and one only hoped that she knew how to look after herself; it would be too hideously embarrassing if she became pregnant and involved you in all the mess and expense of an abortion.

I did not realize then that I feared and distrusted women: feared them because they could reject me and expose me to mortification of defeat, and mistrusted them because I did not understand them. And so I alternated between spasms of aggression and shyness, and all the middle ground of liking and tenderness was lost. It was no wonder I was rebuffed. I actually reached the age of twenty-one before I managed to get a girl to consent. The encounter took place on a rubbish heap on an empty block of land beside her parents' house, and was not very successful since she infected me with a mild form of venereal disease—a wry joke to look back on now but it seemed cataclysmic at the time. It confirmed my belief that women were both predatory and dangerous.

Why is it that my mind goes harking back to these dismal interludes? Is it a form of conceit, a way of saying, 'Look at me now. See how far I have come from my wretched beginnings?' I do not know. All I am saying is that a block forms in my mind when I think about my youth; somehow it was wrong, it ought to have been different. Yet it really wasn't as wretched as all that. By the end of my third year at the university I was doing rather well. I had taken my degree as a bachelor of arts, I had my group of friends whom I saw every day, and there was even talk of making me editor of the university magazine. Moreover, I had managed to get into the hockey team, and had been given a half-blue. The depression was lifting at last and financially I was doing rather well. The weekly column for *Table Talk* had now been exchanged for a regular job reporting news for the *Herald* every day, which was much more profitable, and with what passionate interest I opened the paper each evening and counted the number of lines that had been printed under some such headline as 'Students' Rag. Beehive in Classroom.' A third of a column, worth seven shillings and ninepence.

At the end of my second year I had had an unbelievable piece of good luck. It was the established practice for the examination results, which were long lists of the successful candidates' numbers, to be published in the morning papers. These lists, I discovered, were available at the university registrar's office in the early afternoon, and I asked the chief of staff of my paper if he would like to publish them in his final edition, which came out about five o'clock in the evening. He said he would. Accordingly, on the following day, I picked up the lists—a thick sheaf of typewritten numbers—and made off post-haste to the *Herald* office. There was just time to catch the last edition before it went to press, and it was with much satisfaction that I saw the result of my efforts an hour or two later:

two solid columns of type. The question was, what were they going to pay me? I had written nothing, had acted simply as a messenger boy; still, I was entitled to some sort of reward and I decided that £2 a week was a reasonable sum, plus my tram fares. Without mentioning the £2 I took the matter up with the chief-of-staff at the end of the week, and he told me that he would have to consult the editor. I was to return on the following day. He was a little brusque when I reached his office next evening. 'I'm sorry,' he said, 'we can only give you the usual 2½d. a line. You will have to be satisfied with that.'

I can fairly say that no rewards that have come to me in later life—not Lord Beaverbrook's handsome emoluments, nor literary prizes, nor all the largesse of book royalties or trans-Atlantic film rights—have given me quite the same pleasure as this tremendous pronouncement from the Melbourne *Herald*'s chief-of-staff. I went out into the street too dazed and elated to know where I was going, and at the same time gnawed by a terrible fear that there must have been some mistake, I could not have heard correctly. But no, the cheque arrived. In that first week I made £17 10s. 0d., and since the examinations' results continued to come out for three weeks and were followed by a further set of examinations later in the year, my financial future was assured.

I was not at all eager to come down from the university, and this windfall decided me to try for a law degree, which meant an additional couple of years. It was not a very sensible step to take—I never really intended to abandon writing for the law—but I had slipped into a safe and re-assuring routine and this was a way of putting off for a little longer that testing moment when one would have to enter the hard world outside. I had my favourite seat in the library, I knew what lectures I could safely skip, I had my daily game of billiards in the clubhouse, and the hockey; I edited the magazine, I pursued a girl or two,

2

and in the holidays I went off to a sheep station in the Riverina or surfed on the beaches of the southern coast.

What did I learn? Certainly nothing I can remember now about Torts or Copyright or Equity or Property. Of Latin hardly a phrase remains. I was no scholar, but rather one of the many students who bone up subjects, liking some, hating others, for the purpose of passing examinations, and who then promptly and gratefully forgot all about them. One thing however the university did teach me, and that was vital—the technique of how to learn. I found this useful many years later when finally I settled down to read history of my own accord and discovered that I could concentrate with an absorption which would never have been possible without an academic training.

Naturally I grew bored during these last two years at the University—I was over-staying my time—but I did not realize this until I was actually sitting for my final examinations. Then out of nowhere and very unexpectedly the light of reason descended. I had gone into the examination hall and had begun to answer a paper on Modern Political Institutions when suddenly I saw with absolute clarity that this was all nonsense: I would never make a lawyer. What I had to do was to get up and go out of the hall and take a tram down to the offices of the *Herald*. And there I would apply for a job as a full-time reporter. No one was allowed to leave before the half-hour bell sounded, and there I sat with the empty foolscap before me waiting for some inner voice to say, 'Don't be a fool. You can't throw up your degree like this.' But no voice spoke. At the first peal of the bell I was making my way past the bent heads of the other candidates and the mutely accusing glances of the invigilators, and I had a feeling of great elation as I rode down to the city. What I would have done if I had not got the job I do not know; but I did get it and I went to work on the following day.

Journalism came naturally to me. I rejoiced in the sour smell of printers' ink as an actor rejoices in grease-paint. I never failed to open the paper and see a story I had written without inwardly gloating: 'Look. This is mine. I wrote it.' Even if it was no more than a paragraph at the bottom of an inside page the effect was always the same: I was in print, I was a professional, I was being paid for a personal act of creation. My technical qualifications for newspaper work were not very good. I had no visual memory for words and consequently I could not spell; to this day I do not know whether it is 'yatch' or 'yacht' without looking up the word in the dictionary. I never could learn shorthand and I still type with three fingers. On the other hand, I had a nose for news, the trick of knowing just what will interest people and attract attention. In some ways too my lack of shorthand was an advantage, since it forced me to concentrate and develop a short-term memory. I soon found that I could come away from an interview and remember with pretty fair accuracy everything that had been said; and this was useful since people talk more freely if you do not take notes.

For a year or two I was kept on minor routine jobs— there was a grisly six months when I attended the daily inquests at the morgue—and then more interesting work began to come my way. I was not much good at crime or politics. But acts of God, floods, bushfires, shipwrecks and plagues of locusts, those were the things for me. Away one would go with a photographer in a car or a little chartered plane, and it was a marvellous thing to see a mountainside on fire with balls of flame rushing through the tree-tops, or wooden shacks floating like toys down a flooded valley, or the great southerly waves beating on a stranded ship. Then one could spread one's wings. Then the words came thick and fast. I would cling to the telephone in some little country post office and dictate my prose to a stenographer in the *Herald* office; 'Only one man has survived this night of terror and he told me this graphic story in the hospital late this afternoon . . .' NIGHT OF TERROR ran the headline on the front page that night, and beneath it a glorious spread of print, a column at least, and more again on the inside pages. All of it from Our Special Correspondent.

I must have thrown myself into this sort of work with some gusto for I was frequently given out of town assignments as my days with the *Herald* went on, and my salary crept up from £4 a week to £7 or £8. I soon found friends among the other reporters, since journalists tend to cling together. In a sense they opt out of normal life because they choose to write about it, and so they regard themselves as an esoteric group set apart from the rest of society. Among themselves they talk almost entirely about news and newspapers in much the same way as actors will talk only of the theatre and of themselves. Almost every morning half a dozen of us would meet at a coffee-house before we scattered over the town on our assignments, and we met again in the pubs in the evening when the day's work was done. Nearly all of us were left wing, and we glowed with hate for Mussolini and the up and coming Hitler. We read such books as John Reed's *Ten Days that Shook the World* and Sholokov's *And Quiet Flows the Don* (though I personally preferred Ernest Hemingway), and some of us joined the Writers' League which had affiliations with the communist party. Every one of us I suspect was secretly either planning or already working on a novel.

All this was a pleasant carry-over from my university days, and I think for once I must have been moderately content. And yet not quite. I yearned to go abroad, to get to the centre of things and events that I had been hearing about at secondhand all my life. Probably the others had the same ambition too, but with me it was an obsession. I began to put aside every penny that I could spare and I decided that directly I had £500 I would escape—at first to London and then why not the whole world? That was my plan and soon I began to think of almost nothing else. At last in May 1936 I got away. I was almost twenty-six.

To the Edgware Road   II

DURING THOSE early days of 1940 in Cairo it amused other people that Alex and I were so much together, for we were the most complete of opposites. If you found an epithet for Alex then its antithesis almost certainly applied to me. I was short, he was large. He was shy, precise and disillusioned. I was aggressive, erratic and full of enthusiasms. I cannot think that we fundamentally altered each other's natures, but as time went by it is certainly true that I absorbed a little of his precision, his reticence and his quite extraordinarily cerebral approach to life. And perhaps he on his side found in me many of the things that were wanting in himself, a sense of practical direction and the power to take decisions, a certain eagerness and gregariousness. Then too it must have given him both confidence and satisfaction to correct and instruct so wildly inaccurate and illiterate a mind as mine was. In return for this right of patronage he was usually quite willing to follow my lead however capricious and illogical it might have seemed to him to be.

For me, an Australian, with the habit of making quick and superficial friendships, the gradual deepening of our relationship was not a very difficult process. For Alex, with a more complicated European background, it was not so easy. He had more to commit and he was filled with the memory of disappointments. I recall one day our laughing over the anecdote about Lord Macaulay's precosity at the age of three or four—the story of how the nurse spilled a basin of boiling water over his foot, and of how, after a time, the child reassured the distraught woman: 'Thank you, Madam, the pain is much abated'—

33

but Alex himself seemed to have been just such a prodigy.
Much later on his mother told me that he was scarcely five
when he first played Bach on the piano, and it was also
about that time that she had given him an atlas. Within a
few hours he handed it back to her saying that he had read
it, by which he meant that he was now able from memory
to draw every map in the book.

Later too I saw a photograph of Alex as a schoolboy,
and there was something Billy-Bunterish about him, with
his owl-like spectacles, plump cheeks and his solemn
studious air. It did not seem to me that he could have been
very popular at school; this was the face of the boy who
knew all the answers and was always, smugly, top of the
form. And in fact he had won scholarships which had taken
him through Charterhouse and Oxford. He seemed to
have absorbed every fact they taught him with a cold,
analytical attention. Logic was his passion, and because he
had a sensitive ear most languages, dead and modern,
came to him easily. He had also studied mathematics and
history with that same persistent and practical curiosity.
In some ways it was a magpie brain; he gathered facts as
some philatelists will collect stamps, not through any
aesthetic or cultural motive, but because the facts were
valuable in themselves; and he could never bear to be
wrong or ignorant. There had not been much money in his
family, but he had contrived to go to the winter sports in
Austria before the war, and he had travelled third class or
on a bicycle over a good deal of Europe, steadily accumulat-
ing more facts, more languages, more knowledge of
everything from painting to cooking.

After Oxford there had been an anti-climax; he had
taken a job as a night sub-editor at Reuters, and had lived
very simply for some years in back rooms in London
(Reuters were notorious for their low salaries). Finally
they had sent him to Spain, and later to Germany. This,
then, was the walking dictionary, the precise, diffident,

unpolitical and unambitious man whom I had first met at
the Bar Basque at St Jean de Luz. He was a journalist by
accident, for he was not more interested in writing than in
half a dozen other occupations. He learned it as he had
learned pingpong or the differential calculus. He had no
flair—just a cool appraisal of the technique.

I do not really know what it was that kept us together
through these first days in Cairo, when we had as yet done
nothing more than present the surfaces of our personali-
ties to one another, and each of us could easily have made
other friends. Probably the real mainspring of our friendship was the war; it isolated us from our past lives. We
were like two strangers who cling together in a shipwreck.

I think we began to see this clearly for the first time one
day when we were dangling our legs in the Gezira
swimming pool. Behind us in the clubhouse Egyptian
waiters wearing white gowns, red cummerbunds and
fezes were laying out the buffet luncheon. Crows and
kites swooped past the tables in search of unguarded
morsels of food, and in the gardens beyond the date palms
rustled in the midday breeze coming off the Nile. Beyond
this again Egypt vanished and was replaced by the im-
memorial prospects of an English country summer day;
the frieze of cricketers in white flannels and the tennis
players, the nursemaids walking with their prams, the
golfers with their caddies, the green grass, the atmosphere
of indefinite, indolent leisure in a greenish-yellow light;
in short, an English garrison scene which was then
familiar enough all the way from Singapore to Egypt. For
some days past the news from France had been getting
worse and worse. Now, as we drank Pimm's No. 1 and
listened to the club wireless we heard that Sedan in France
had fallen, and suddenly it became apparent that this scene
around us was unreal, unreal in the sense that it was
already out of date and doomed. The fall of France was the

2*

end of the world as we had known it up till then and the beginning of something different, a more dangerous, infinitely harsher, existence. The liner had ceased sailing along in a calm sea and the shipwreck had arrived.

There was a moment of repining and helpless fear in Cairo. We were far away; we thought we were ruined without so much as being able to make a gesture of defence. Alex could see no possibility of Britain holding out. He had spent a year in Germany in 1938 and 1939 (he came out of Berlin in the last train), and was one of the few Englishmen who knew that most of the British propaganda about the Nazis was rubbish; the Germans were fanatically loyal, determined and ruthless. He asserted now that the British army in France could not retreat to Spain, nor could it hope to be evacuated from the channel ports. Soon Hitler would invade England and the British would surrender. His reasoning was right, of course, but his logic made no allowance for the unexpected reservoirs of human courage or for the stupidity of others—in this case the stupidity of Hitler, who prevented Guderian's panzer divisions from scooping in the British expeditionary force at Dunkirk before it was evacuated. Perhaps too he was unusually gloomy that day because he was more bound up with Europe than I was. After all, it was barely four years since I had seen England for the first time.

Katherine

When I came to England in 1936 one of my companions
on the voyage was a boy named Frank Sullivan with
whom I had been friendly at the university. He really had
wretched luck; he dressed himself up as a fairy for the
fancy dress ball in the Red Sea, and he grew very heated
as he danced the Black Bottom and the Charleston. Then
he made the mistake of cooling off on deck in his flimsy
costume. Half way up the Mediterranean he took to his
bed, and by the time we passed through the Straits of
Gibraltar his illness was diagnosed as pneumonia. At that
time there were no antibiotics to cope with the disease; it
rose steadily to a crisis and on the ninth day the patient
either died or made a rapid recovery. In the Bay of Biscay
it seemed quite likely that Frank would die, and the ship
was diverted to Plymouth so that he could be landed and
taken to hospital. A launch came out to meet us in the
harbour and he was lowered into it on a stretcher. I
followed down the gangway feeling very conscious of the
doleful faces of the hundreds of other passengers lining the
rails.

It was a dismal ending to all my expectations of a gay
and exciting arrival in England, but the staff at the nursing
home were very kind; they even provided a bed for me so
that I could be called if Frank died in the night, and I felt a
little less alone with my responsibility after I had got off
a carefully worded cable to Frank's family in Melbourne.
Then I set out on foot to inspect the town. Up to this
point I had hardly noticed my new surroundings, but now I
did take note, now I looked around and unconsciously
compared my preconceived notions of what England

would be like with what was actually before my eyes. It is a very fragile and fortuitous thing, this moment of the first impression, but with me it is indelible, and no matter whether I am dealing with places or people I seldom altogether forget it or perhaps see so clearly again. I walked down a steep street towards the centre of the town, and it was marvellous to me that the houses could be so closely huddled together, terrace after terrace, all alike, all so cosy, so regimented, so unnautical. I myself was nautical. After four weeks at sea the ground rose and fell gently beneath my feet, and my dreams of Plymouth were of smoke-wreathed cannon and of Drake and Nelson setting out in their glory from Plymouth Hoe—not these grey and sober houses with their complacent chimneypots. Those canary birds in the bay windows should have been oath-screeching parrots. Yet there was a solidity here, an earth-based I-am-what-I-am-ness, that was reassuring.

I turned into a park with iron railings around it. Why railings? There were no railings around our parks; they were as open as the bush. And then arrived my moment of mild revelation. I found myself in front of the green and mossy bole of an immense tree that spread out its dense foliage some forty feet above my head. I stood there in the gentle rain and studied this object with close attention, for I had never seen such a thing before. It was the dampest and greenest tree in the whole world. I reached forward and felt the clammy smoothness of the trunk, I picked up a piece of moss from between the tangled roots, and I gazed upward at the thick canopy of leaves above, the abode no doubt of Squirrel Nutkin and a suitable hiding-place for Robin Hood. My Australian eye was adjusted to thin grey leaves with hard sunshine in between and the hard dry plain beyond, and now, by contrast, this explosion of lushness and greenness was delightful. It enveloped one, hid one away, gave one a sense of lazy virility. And in the same way the warm and gentle rain enveloped one and so

did the terraced houses. It was the harmony of suburbia
and the jungle, a painting by the Douanier Rousseau.
Later on in London I grew to detest the warm and gentle
rain, and I longed for the sun and a distant view, but I
never got tired of the greenness, and still after thirty years
or more it is impossible for me to think of England without
some gadget in my brain turning a light upon a long row
of houses all alike, and a burst of jungle greenery dividing
them from the street.

When Frank recovered and we went up to London I had
a similar experience among the crowds, the first per-
manent crowds I had ever known. I loved the march of
faceless strangers in the street. To be known by no one,
watched by no one, to join in the ant-like anonymous
procession—this was a new and exhilarating kind of
privacy. Somewhere in his *Voyage au bout de la nuit* which
I was reading at that time Ferdinand Celine says that he
screamed and yelled out of the open window of his bedroom when he reached New York, but no one heard him,
and he was made frantic by that indifference. I did not
feel like yelling at all in London. We had rooms in
Bloomsbury, in Mecklenburg Square (25s. a week for
bed and breakfast), we ate in Lyons cornerhouses, we
drank in the Fleet Street pubs, and we were a part of the
town.

Perhaps best of all was the feeling I had that at last I
was in the centre of the world instead of being on the
periphery; you could observe events with your own eyes as
they were happening instead of forever hearing about
them at secondhand. Here was Edward VIII proposing to
abdicate and you could actually see him driving out of
Buckingham Palace and find in the paper a photograph of
Mrs Simpson that had been taken that very day. It was
not too difficult to get into the House of Commons and
hear Anthony Eden making a speech about the Nyon
Agreement, and the Spanish Civil War itself was only a

day's journey away. If you wanted to see young Laurence Olivier making his first appearance in *Hamlet* there he was in the Old Vic just across the river; and if you were in funds you could nip across the channel to Paris and go to the *Folies Bergère* where Josephine Baker was executing her celebrated dance wearing nothing but a girdle of bananas round her waist.

Then too there was the feeling that one was entirely free, one could go anywhere and do anything. Soon after I arrived in London I met a young South African journalist named Guy Young, and like myself he had come to London with a few hundred pounds in his pocket. We decided that we should make a journey on the continent together, and we went into the Lyons Cornerhouse in Ludgate Circus to discuss the matter. At the door we bought a copy of the *Evening Standard* and on the front page there was a paragraph with the heading 'Riots in Spain'. Without another thought we started making plans. Guy knew an American correspondent in Burgos to whom he could apply for a temporary job. I had a friend in one of the news agencies in Fleet Street and I went off there at once to see if he would commission me to do a series of articles on Spain. This was how I met Katherine.

She was sitting in the outer office of the news agency where she worked as a typist. I gave her the name of the man I wanted to see and then found myself saying, 'Will you have dinner with me tonight?'

'No,' she said, 'I can't do that.'

'Then tomorrow night?'

'I'm sorry—not tomorrow either.'

I got my commission for the articles, and when I came out from the interview I said, 'This may be the last chance. I am going to Spain tomorrow.'

She shook her head.

'I may be killed. I may never come back.'

No response.

'If I do come back will you have dinner with me?'

She smiled at last. 'Perhaps,' she said. 'We'll see.'

That first journey across Europe is still very vivid to me now. It was the holiday period when the crowds were making their way south, but this did not matter to Guy and me in the least, in fact we enjoyed the confusion. We crossed on the Golden Arrow to Paris and then made our way to the Gare Quai d'Orsay to take the overnight train to the Spanish border. Who will ever forget his first sight of a pre-war French railway terminus at the rush hour? The porters in blue smocks and cloth caps careering by with agitated families in their wake, the loudspeakers booming *En voiture s'il vous plaît*, the locomotive hissing steam like a great beast impatient to be off, the bulbous French mothers with chalk-faced, black-eyed babies who screamed and screamed, and the frantic cries of the little darting fathers.

Not for us the sleeping-car. We found a place on a wooden bench in a third-class compartment and bought ourselves little loaves with slabs of ham inside and a bottle of wine. Then a bell clanged and we were on our way. The compartment was preposterously overcrowded and already the atmosphere was thick with the smells of sweat and garlic and cheap tobacco. It billowed against the shut windows and there congealed in a film on the glass. As we ran through the Paris suburbs a ticket collector heaved himself painfully from compartment to compartment along the carriage. '*Messieurs, 'dames. Vos billets s'il vous plaît.*' Standing there in the doorway being shoved and pushed by the people in the corridor he was wonderfully polite.

Inch by inch the woman next to me expanded along the wooden bench. She was an exceptionally fat woman dressed in black with a purple shawl, and I could feel the flesh of her buttocks creeping along the seat towards me. On her lap was a sleeping baby and a bunch of bananas.

Her husband sat beside her reading the newspaper *Paris Soir* and breathing clouds of tobacco smoke into the air. Three nuns, rosaries in hand, sat on the opposite bench making themselves as inconspicuous as possible, and beside them were two young men with red scarves round their necks and cloth caps down on their eyes. Strange advertisements flashed by on the lighted stations. 'Dubo . . . Dubon . . . Dubonnet.' What was it? Soap? The name of a car? There were several commotions in the night; once when the nuns got out at a wayside station and there was a stampede for their seats among the people standing in the corridor; once again when the two young men in red scarves began quarrelling; and a third time when the baby woke, coughed, and broke into a high-pitched scream. Its mother pulled her left breast out of her dress and stifled the noise with her nipple.

Feeling thirsty and stiff I squirmed myself out of the compartment and made my way to the lavatory, where there were many slips of yellow paper lying about, and the stench of carbolic and urine rose up from a hole in the floor. I was beset with misgivings. What was the point of our going to Spain? What were we going to do there? Had someone stolen our suitcases which we had left at the end of the corridor? Would we pass our stop? How were we going to get anyone to understand us since we spoke no Spanish? Why hadn't I stayed in London and got to know that wonderful girl?

When I got back to the compartment Guy had fallen asleep with his head on his neighbour's shoulder and I pushed my way down beside him.

I woke in the morning when the first warm shaft of sunshine travelled up my legs, growing wider and more yellow and warmer as it advanced, until it struck me full on the face. My skin felt like parchment and the faces of the other passengers were lined and dirty and tired. And yet, despite the foetid air, the chaotic mess and staleness of the compartment and the dryness of my throat, all my anxieties of the night before flew away. There was a rush of bright green foliage outside, and this, as I rubbed my eyes, resolved itself into fields of hop poles strung with necklaces of green leaves, and tall bamboos, and red and yellow roofs of cordova tiles, and donkeys with spilling bags of carrots and onions on their backs, and beyond all this the clear racing blue of the Atlantic. It was a lovely day.

When we got to the border at Hendaye they would not let us cross into Spain: the frontier was closed. We did not take this very seriously; in those July days of 1936 few of us had the slightest notion of what lay ahead. Later on the issues became brutally clear and people took sides with a passionate conviction, but for us, at this moment, it was 'Riots in Spain', that was all. On the long flat beach at Hendaye only a mile or two away from the fighting the French children played with their buckets and spades just as they had always done every summer. For Guy and myself it was all rather a spree; we were simply annoyed at not being able to get over the border in much the same way as we might have been annoyed at not getting into a bullfight.

And in fact we did get in. It was rather a silly adventure but it seemed exhilarating at the time. After a day or two we bought a secondhand motorcycle and made for a little frontier post called Dancharia, which was further inland. It was a sleepy place, especially in the middle of the day, and farm carts were still passing into Spain. We waited until the barriers were lifted to let one by and then we raced through before anyone could stop us. The road was empty. In a few minutes we were roaring away up into the Pyrenees and that night we got to Pamplona. The pro-Franco Carlists had taken over the town and there was a great come and go of the military in the plaza. They were stopping and questioning every foreigner in the streets, and it was not long before they picked on us. We were taken before an officer in some sort of a barracks and told very brusquely that we had to get out of Spain at once. We managed to find a pension that would take us in for the night and we would have tried to push on to Burgos on the following day but it was impossible to buy petrol anywhere without a ration card, and every few miles there was a military post on the road.

I don't think we were particularly sorry. Nothing very exciting seemed to be happening anywhere, the food in Pamplona was appalling, and the soldiers forced everyone to stay indoors after dark. It was my twenty-sixth birthday and I wanted to celebrate. 'Let's go to Paris,' I said to Guy. 'We can see the *Folies Bergère* and then perhaps go on to Berlin for the Olympic Games.'

He thought it a good idea. And thus, fecklessly and carelessly, feeling as free as migratory birds, we departed for France. A day or two later we were as much engrossed in watching Josephine Baker dancing in her girdle of bananas as we had been in the civil war. And then we set off for Berlin.

In the summer of 1936 Germany for a few short weeks really was like a tourist poster. The sun shone, the flowers bloomed, every railway-station was bedecked with flags, and saluting policemen were ready to help the foreigner wherever he went. It was rather like being at some provincial féte where everyone smiles, everyone is eager to lend a hand with the refreshments, and goodwill overflows. 'Look,' the Germans seemed to be saying, 'this is what we are really like. Let us all enjoy ourselves.' Then too they were so efficient. Multi-lingual officials boarded the trains coming into Berlin and arranged accommodation for those visitors who had not already booked. The hotels had filled long before Guy and I arrived, but we were provided with a good cheap room in an old lady's apartment in the Sudwestkorso, and the old lady herself was the apotheosis of *gemütlich* German hospitality. And so we sallied out into the festival of brass bands and beer gardens and processions and milling crowds in the Olympic stadium. There was hardly a swastika to be seen on the streets.

And yet the vague menace was there. You felt it lurking underneath all this heartiness and precise attention, and just once in a while it would emerge into the open in some small incident as when a policeman barked savagely at one of his own countrymen and drew his baton, or when Hitler, on the saluting stand at the stadium, refused to shake hands with the American negro Jesse Owens who was the great champion of the games that year. One day when we were on the Unter den Linden a gust of nervous excitement suddenly took possession of the crowds. The people ran to the edge of the pavement, thrusting one another aside in an hysterical, almost frantic kind of way. Hitler was coming. We were talking to a German girl we had picked up and it was astonishing to see the shining-eyed look of ecstasy that overcame her face as the great man came riding by through a forest of outstretched arms. It was the look of a girl meeting her lover.

And the virility of the Germans: this really was a little frightening. The main drive way up to the stadium was lined with statues of the young demi-gods and goddesses of the new Nazi age: great bull-like young men with truculent sexual parts and huge-bellied women carrying sheaves of wheat. There they stood flexing their muscles and gazing with calm animal strength away to the horizon. There was something mildly shocking about them. Those vast stone breasts did not charm the eye at all, they simply suggested that they were full of good milk. And those mountainous buttocks were an obvious makeweight for a gargantuan pregnancy, which would not be long delayed: one tigerish spring from the naked athlete standing opposite and the job would be done.

But then we were all in a daze of body-worship through these days. One afternoon Guy and I went out to the Olympischdorf, where the Germans had laid out a country club to accommodate the Olympic teams. We passed through heavy iron gates—only men allowed—and from then on we were surrounded by lakes and flowers and well-regimented forests of spruce and fir. The athletes lived in rustic log-cabins among the woods, and there were enough cinder-tracks, swimming pools and gymnasia to train themselves until they burst. Each team hoisted its national flag over the log-cabin in which it was stabled—I say stabled because the whole thing was conducted like a model racing stud. Swarms of little men in white sweaters and sandshoes and with white towels over their shoulders frisked about the athletes every minute of the day, polishing their skins, kneading their muscles, feeding them special foods and leading them back to their wooden boxes at night. There was a preposterous earnestness about it all and the air reeked with the smell of liniment and human sweat. Let one of the young gods so much as trip over a step or complain of a sore toe on the race-track and the trainers were round him in a second, tenderly inquiring where it hurt; and that look of maternal concern on their horny faces was something that went beyond caricature.

Soothing music brooded over the valley, and everything possible was done to keep away the vulgarities of the outside world. The athlete's mail was censored. No tradesman's van was allowed inside these precincts, no crowds, no sudden alarming noises. Life went by in an idyllic dream of rusticity and simplicity until that electric moment when the athlete was taken off in a padded car to perform for a brief minute or two before the crowds; and then, directly his event was over, he was whisked back to compose himself and resume his dedicated austerity.

We arrived soon after breakfast, and for a while we

talked in low earnest voices with some of the members of the American team whom Guy knew. Then we were conducted to an astonishing spectacle; the Swedish baths. This was a wooden building beside a swimming pool, and for a moment on entering one could see very little because the place was enveloped in thick and sweet-smelling steam. Then my eyes adjusted themselves, and I made out an immense metal stove lying against the whole of one wall. Into this from time to time an attendant hurled large logs of Swedish pine. Directly the wood caught he played a fire-hose into the blaze, and resinous steam came billowing out into the room like smoke from a factory chimney.

Opposite the stove, a series of wide wooden benches rose up in tiers to the ceiling as in a university lecture hall. Upon these some twenty or thirty young men of many different nationalities were lying. They lay like seals on a rocky coast, stark naked, indolent, sleek and beautiful, and one's first impression was of some vast Cinquecento canvas crowded with major and minor angels, except that this was an adoration not of the spirit but of the flesh. They fell into natural groups of twining limbs and torsos, and there were some like Michelangelo's Adam on the ceiling of the Sistine Chapel, with tiny neat heads and huge, reposing, sexless bodies, others rounded and ardent like Tintoretto's young Bacchus, others like tall and sinewy El Grecos, or mild and fluid like Correggio's men. Every few minutes one or two of the forms would lazily change position and so create a new grouping and a new suggestion of a masterpiece.

All this we observed through that pall of blue steam which softened every outline, and by some chemistry made every colour slightly luminous. Guy and I like everyone else, had taken off our clothes to enter this sanctuary, and feeling embarrassed and puny we stepped up to the nearest bench to take our place among these, the strongest, the swiftest, the healthiest and most beautifully proportioned young men in the countries of the world.

After ten minutes we had had enough. The attendant who handed us our towels as we came out was English. 'Want a rub down?' he asked.

While I lay on the table he discoursed on his work. 'I rub them when they come to that Swedish Turkey bath,' he said. He scooped out a sponge from a pail of water and put it on the spot where I could least endure that icy cold.

'Is that absolutely necessary?' I asked.

'Don't suppose it is for you, being a visitor. But for them others'—he jerked a thumb towards the bathhouse, 'they haven't been allowed near a woman for weeks and they're that highly trained you can hardly lay a finger on 'em. It's being in the pink of condition that does it. I have this sponge in and out of the water half a dozen times with some of them before I'm through. God knows what happens when they come out of training. But' (he removed the sponge and turned me over on my stomach) 'I expect a young feller like you on the loose in Berlin gets his fun all right.'

We got dressed and walked rather light-headedly out into the sunshine. It was noon, and already a group of German girls had gathered at the iron gates. They were peering avidly through the grill-work at the human stallions parading about on the green lawn beside the lake. I had then a sudden memory of the Australian sheep-station to which I used to go for my holidays. The wool was carted across the plains to the railway by a team of fourteen huge Clydesdale mares, and each year, when the shearing was over, it was the custom for a stallion to be placed among these mares so that they would foal in the following year. On this particular day that I now re-membered so clearly the mares, on returning from the railway, saw the stallion from far off, and they reared and tossed against their harness in great excitement. By the

time we reached the yards they were almost unmanage-
able; we wrestled, cursing, with their heavy leather collars
while the stallion stood nonchalantly by affecting not to
notice. Then finally the harness was clear at last, and the
mares, with their great rumps frisking in the air, went
neighing up to the stallion. And now at last he noticed
them. He lifted his shaggy forelegs and set off at a gallop
towards the open country with the mares thundering after
him. We saw them streaming up to the horizon in the
evening light, manes and tails flying in the wind, their
heads held high, their necks arched, and they were bunched
together and travelling at tremendous speed with the
stallion still in front. I remembered too, the next morning, when they came back, all fourteen of them and the
stallion, and they stood with calm eyes, listlessly and
quietly cropping the grass. And thus no doubt the athletes
would have run from these German girls had they
managed to get in through the gates.

I am, I suspect, making rather too much of these scenes
in Berlin, just as I have made too much of the green tree at
Plymouth and the journey down to the Spanish border.
They do not form a coherent pattern. Yet these are the
pictures I would have painted had I been an impressionist,
these are the things that I remember, and they have a
place in my late education. At this time I was still in the
stage of sticking labels on to places and people and events,
and I was very much the victim of my own haphazard
experiences. I still did not want to pause and understand
what I was observing so much as I wanted to go on and on
seeing new places and meeting new people. Above all I
did not yet want to commit myself, to accept responsibility, to take up attitudes which I would have to defend.
I was indignant at what was happening in Spain but not
sufficiently so to make me feel that I ought to join the
International Brigade. I had liked England on sight but I
liked travelling more. I was nagged by the feeling that I

should have arrived in Europe at least five years earlier, and that now there was not much time left, that war was bound to come or that revolutions would break out or some other catastrophe would intervene and shut me off from these strange and famous places before I had had a chance to know them. No doubt I was also haunted by the usual young man's fear that all too soon I would be incarcerated in one place by a job, by marriage, by the inertia of a network of comfortable habits. I was not really lazy or restless or irresponsible; I was simply enjoying my freedom and I was not ready to go home. Even my literary ambitions seemed to have been drained out of me for the time being.

So now when the Olympic games were over I would have made my way south to Italy and then perhaps to the Balkans, even Russia, but it was no good; the money was running out. I had no choice but go to back to London and try to find a job.

Directly I had set myself up again in Mecklenburg Square I went round to Katherine's office.

'Now will you say yes?'

'Yes.'

'Tonight?'

'All right.'

And so it began. It seems a little unfair to drag Katherine too deeply into this record—after all, I was only an incident in her life—and yet I cannot think of this period when I really began to know England without relating it to her. She haunts the scene no matter where I focus my memory, she stands there in the foreground, she is part of the view. She walks towards me at our place of rendezvous outside the Criterion brasserie in Piccadilly Circus where a hansom cab used to stand, and then we are in the foyer of the Gaiety Theatre in Aldwych where the Blackbirds of 1936 are playing, and we are riding in a bus down Fleet Street, and hanging over the wall on the

embankment at Westminster, and sitting facing one
another in twenty different little restaurants in Soho and
Chelsea, and then we are coming back to the not-so-clean
bed-sitting room in Mecklenburg Square late at night. She
peels off her stockings and unhooks her belt with a quick
decisive air and I feel that I am a very fine chap indeed.

She was about to marry a man to whom she was very
much beholden. He was the lover who is also the father-
figure. For a long time he had given himself up to her,
had cherished her, had forgiven her (there was much to
forgive), and he had taught her, she said, everything she
knew. She on her side was devoted to him, but just for the
moment she was having a last fling with me—well, perhaps fling is not quite the right word for it: what she was
really doing was engaging in a little Pygmalionism of her
own. Here was this eager boy from Australia who seemed
to know so little about the world, not even the fact that he
had a cockney accent. What fun to educate him, to be herself a teacher, just for a while, to take him to the theatres,
the galleries and the restaurants, and perhaps in return to
feel a little of the glow of his enthusiasm. This last was a
vital part of our relationship, just as it was to be later with
Alex. I do not want to pose as a young innocent who went
about bringing light and hope into other people's jaded
lives—I was not so innocent as all that—but I do think I
was able to rouse Katherine a little out of her despair.

The trouble was that she minded everything so much,
she had a skin too few. She thought the world was sliding
downhill so fast there was no hope for it any more. She
was the sort of person who cannot hear about a famine in
Bengal without feeling that she personally is responsible
and ought to do something about it. She could never resist
a beggar in the street. And while she cared so much about
other people she was utterly reckless with herself. All her
instinct was to give, wildly, impulsively and with everything she had. She wanted to be all things to all men and

women all the time and to save nothing for herself. I suppose this made her into a bit of a tramp, and certainly she was impossible to live with since she was too gregarious to be loyal to any one person for very long. But she didn't at all look like a tramp. She had a petite, rather boyish figure, a turned-up nose, and she was very very pretty—the prettiest girl I had ever seen. I was not usually a ready giver, but just to look at her made me want to buy her flowers, and to trot around beside her and to do whatever she wanted to do. She had no notion of time at all, mostly because she always got swept away by what she was doing at the moment. I would get more and more resentful as I waited beside that hansom cab in Piccadilly, saying to myself over and over again, 'She can't have forgotten. I will give her just ten more minutes'; and then, of course, another ten; and when she did appear at last I could not bring myself to complain, I was just overwhelmingly pleased to see her.

I don't say that I altogether surrendered my independence—I was far too selfish for that—but she gave me a feeling of naturalness I had never had with a girl before, and I felt a little lost if she vanished, as she frequently did, for a week or two. I knew she was out with other men, but I didn't care; I wanted her back again.

We could only meet on those evenings when she found some plausible excuse to give to her fiancé and I suppose by present standards it was rather a tame affair, mostly a matter of just talking in pubs. Very occasionally we managed to get away for the weekend, and I remember one particularly happy time when we walked around Stonehenge in the snow and then came back to a warm hotel bedroom in Salisbury. Oh, the pleasure of the chintz-covered double bed and the drawn chintz curtains and nobody knowing that we were there. Just for once I had her entirely to myself, far away from her fiancé and her friends in London, and in the manner of Porphyria's lover

(Browning was a great favourite of mine at that time) I might have strangled her had I loved her enough.

But to tell the truth I had no wish to marry her. By this time I had got a job with an Australian news agency in Fleet Street, but I regarded it only as a stopgap, something to tide me over till I could start travelling again, and I certainly did not want to be encumbered with a wife. Besides, there might be other girls. What I did not realize was that I was becoming much more involved than I knew, not only with Katherine, but with all the way of life to which she was introducing me. Little by little under her guidance I was beginning to change my spots and take on the camouflage and the colours of Europe. Despite myself a network of new habits was entwining itself around me, and it was not unpleasant. I began to identify myself with the events that were happening around me: I minded very much about the abdication. I was all in favour of Edward taking a morganatic wife, and I objected strongly to the sanctimonious way in which Baldwin and the Archbishop of Canterbury were manoeuvring him off the throne.

And now at last Spain started to make imperative claims. It was impossible to remain neutral. The blood rushed to the head when some arrogant bully-boy of the right asserted that Franco was simply doing his duty by putting down a lot of blood-thirsty revolutionaries in the pay of Stalin—one wanted to take him by the throat. A young Canadian friend of mine, David Holmested, came into my office one day and said he was off to join an ambulance unit on the Republican side, and I was torn with guilt when I found I could not bring myself to go with him. It was only partly cowardice that kept me back, I think. I never really wanted to fight either in this war or the world war that followed. I was a professional recorder of events, a propagandist, not a soldier. I wanted to be there, to take part in the battle, but only as an observer.

Like most nomads I hovered in the half-world of only partial commitment to religion, to causes, to women and to places, and thus, by definition, to life itself. This is not the stuff out of which you can make either traitors or heroes; it simply leaves you with sensations of frustration and of shallow guilt, which to avoid, you keep moving on.

And of course I had great fun in London that winter. I moved into rather grander quarters in the Gloucester Road (bed and breakfast 35s. a week), I took wine with my meals at the Rendezvous Restaurant across the street, I shared a car with a friend, and talking fiercely in the pubs was a substitute for action. It was a waiting time, a delaying for something I could not quite define, and it was only in the spring that a crisis, like some great dark bird, came winging its way towards me. Katherine announced that her marriage had been fixed for the following week. That did the trick. All at once I realized that I could not let her go, not now, not so soon, not like this. No, it was impossible. She must not do it. 'Listen,' I said, 'the *Bremen* sails for New York tomorrow. I've enough money for two tickets.'

This was a little reckless but I was still not proposing marriage: this was merely to be another rather flamboyant bolt into the blue. Katherine, of course, saw this quite clearly. She might have pushed me to the point of marriage; yes, I believe she could have done that. But she was a giver, not a taker or a demander, and no doubt she realized that marriage required at least one stable character to make it work, at least one shepherd; not two gypsies like ourselves. At all events she would not come. But we were quite determined that we should have one final night together on the night of the eve of her wedding. It really was tremendously gay. We moved around Soho from one haunt to another, and then very late we got back to my room. She was to be married in the country at 11 o'clock on the following morning, but she had her little

car and so we could safely be together until dawn, and
this seemed timeless while it lasted. It was snowing quite
heavily when I took her downstairs in the morning and
said goodbye, and the silly girl must have driven very
carelessly, for she put the car into a ditch just outside
London and broke her arm. However, a doctor was found,
the arm was set, and they managed to get her to the altar
on time. Afterwards she set off with her husband for a
three weeks' honeymoon in Switzerland.

And that presumably was that. I don't imagine that I
suffered too badly; I had friends in London and at twenty-
six there is a certain masochistic joy in romantic despair.
But then you could never presume anything with Katherine,
she simply did not act as other people do. After two weeks
in Switzerland she burst in on me again.

'What's happened?'

'Nothing. Two weeks was enough, that's all.'

'Then it's broken up?'

'No. I just wanted to come back and see you.'

'You can't do this.'

'Oh yes I can.'

And of course she could. Somehow she managed it.
From time to time she would re-appear, we would spend a
disordered night together, and then she would be off again.
Had things been left to Katherine this situation might
have gone on for a long time, but my nerves were not as
strong as hers; I could not stand the strain. Her sudden
visitations became more and more upsetting; she was
irresistible but the let-down after she was gone was
demoralizing, and a week or more might go by before I
had a hope of seeing her again. I was sick of my job, sick of
London, and sick of myself, and may even have been a
little ill, if melancholia is an illness. I longed to get away
to Spain and still I dared not trust myself—how would I
behave at the front? Would I run away?

In the end a journalist friend named Noel Monks (how

much I took his kindness for granted at the time) found a way out. His newspaper, the *Daily Express*, needed a temporary correspondent in Gibraltar, and while he knew they would engage a man on the spot if he were available, he also knew they would not go to the expense of sending a man there from England. He solved this dilemma by telling the foreign editor of the paper that he had a friend, a very promising young fellow, who by luck was just about to leave for Gibraltar. An interview with the editor was arranged, the deal was fixed—I was to be guaranteed £5 a week and minor expenses—and with Noel's help I was just able to raise the money for the third class fare by sea. Katherine was out of my life and I was on my way.

To the Edgware Road   III

ALL THROUGH the war, beginning on the day when Sedan fell in France, I found that one never really comprehended a victory or a calamity until long afterwards. One might assess it mentally, one might experience elation or disappointment, but it was only when one began to remember the little things of life that had been won or lost that one began fully to understand.

So now, watching the bright reflections in the swimming pool at Gezira on that day in May 1940, and during the weeks and months that followed, Alex and I gradually became aware of how many threads were broken. We remembered the Bar Basque and the *jambon de Bayonne*, a flat in Knightsbridge, the golf links at Rye, a suitcase of clothes abandoned in Brussels, an uncashed cheque, a letter which would now never arrive, and the Champs Elysées in the evening. These picture-memories were the signposts to the thing we really dreaded, the bombing of England and the possibility of poison gas as well. Quite seriously we expected never to see our families again.

As usual I tried to rouse Alex. I argued that it was possible to cut one's life in two, to put all one's past experiences and attachments behind one and start afresh on a career that was entirely new. Here in the Middle East we would become nomads of some kind, wandering off into Africa or eastward across the desert to Persia, perhaps for years, until the world had settled down again. It had happened to other armies before. But to Alex this was another of my wild, unreal patches of guesswork. He was broken from his roots, and for him the disaster was an accomplished fact, there was no escape from it. We brooded miserably in Cairo for several days after this, and it was a pleasurable relief when we heard that Mussolini and his famous 'eight million bayonets' were coming into the war. Now at last the action in the desert would begin. We set off on the first of many journeys to the front line in Cyrenaica.

Probably there will never be front lines on the grand scale in the world any more. Already they began to vanish in the Second World War when so much death was dealt out from the open sky and the sea; and so often, even in the desert, the enemy was all around one. But still a front existed in one form or another right up to the end of the fighting, and it was the major factor to which everything else reacted. For five years no matter how far we travelled or how many countries we passed through that imaginary wall was always standing there in front of us. It was a moving precipice, it represented the unknown, and it set up a kind of claustrophobia in our minds.

Different people reacted to the front in many different ways, but I don't think Alex and I ever approached it with any other feeling than that of dread. We may have been caught up in the general excitement and wariness there at times, and that may have put an insulation over our fear; but nearly always it was dread and nothing else, and the joy we had in coming away was so great it was like a sudden release from physical pain. Just not to be at the front—that was often the highest delight we could imagine, and for five years we indulged it whenever we could.

In the timing of his reactions Alex was quite different from me. Once committed to the act of going forward I found I could put up a fairly good outward show, and I was eager to arrive. But that was the worst moment for Alex. He hung back. He sat hunched in a corner of the car as we bumped over the desert, morose, shut in on himself and hopeless. When at last we reached the front—and often it took several days—the fog lifted from his mind and he took over the initiative from me. Then he was the leader, he made the decisions, and although he was not one for putting himself unnecessarily into dangerous places I think he was less afraid than I was.

Alex's character gradually underwent a series of changes as the war went on, but this factor—our behaviour in places of danger—remained a constant between us. We had two other companions who often travelled with us during the war: Christopher Buckley, the correspondent of the London *Daily Telegraph*, and Geoffrey Keating of the King's Royal Rifles, who chanced to be freaks in this matter; so far as I could make out they experienced no fear whatever, and many times they appalled us with their foolhardiness and the insane risks they took. Alex and I dragged on behind them, muttering and fretful, but too frightened to lose sight of them lest we should be left on our own. Our main fear was that we should be taken prisoner, and after that we feared wounds, then death. Of course none of this was apparent at the time. We all appeared to be splendid fellows together, and the façade of cheerfulness and willingness never for long broke down in public, or with each other. We kept up the pretence to the end and made a kind of virtue out of it.

The first front in the desert was like no other front at all. It resembled the sea more than anything else. You travelled usually in convoy—in our case a couple of trucks or station wagons—and in Cairo these were equipped as for a voyage with fresh water, fuel and provisions. Often you steered across the featureless landscape by compass, and you constantly scanned the horizon for signs of other vehicles which might be enemies or friends. When a battle was joined the tanks manoeuvred about one another like destroyers at sea, each tank setting up a great smoking trail of dust in its wake.

On this, our first visit to the front along the escarpment

3

at Sallum on the border of Egypt and Cyrenaica, there were very few tanks on either side, and the Italians were probably a good deal more apprehensive than we were. They lay in their forts and at night they scoured the desert with searchlights in the hope of picking up the silhouettes of British infantry patrols. Occasionally a shell came over, splitting the clear desert air with a whirr like a rising partridge, and we ran and lay huddled in our narrow, grave-like slit-trenches when a Savoia aircraft flew overhead. It was colonial warfare, much space, few men, an occasional inconclusive skirmish at dawn or sunset. One side or the other would suddenly advance, seize a wide patch of desert and then voluntarily retire again. It did not matter how much of the desert you occupied, since there were hardly any favoured positions. The desert was nothing, the enemy was all. It was like a disordered game of chess or draughts in which every piece could move in any direction and there were no squares at all and no edges to the board.

This was a very difficult business to write about with any accuracy. In any case the young British commanders were suspicious of war correspondents and none too keen to explain their movements to us. Then if we did discover what was going on, it usually transpired to be nothing more than a battalion marching from one reference point on the map to another. No towns were taken, no civilians were involved, and across the wide, parched landscape there was nothing much to see. From first to last we never 'saw' a battle in the desert. We were simply conscious of a great deal of dust, noise and confusion. The only way we could gather a coherent picture was by driving hard from one headquarters to another, and by picking up the reports from the most forward units as they came through on the radio telephone. Then, when the worst was over, we went forward ourselves to observe the prisoners and the booty and to hear the individual experiences of the soldiers.

Each evening Alex and I and the other war correspondents sat at our typewriters hunting for similes and metaphors to explain all this and I don't think we ever succeeded, not at any rate on a technical plane. And yet the story of the desert war seemed to write itself. There never was a place which so moved one to composition. Within an hour of arriving in the desert ideas came crowding into one's mind, and if there was no action for days together it made no difference. Life there was so completely abnormal that the first element of a newspaper story was always present: the element of contrast, the spectacle of familiar people (in this case the soldiers) reacting to a strange place. But the real reason why the war correspondents did rather better in the desert than anywhere else was because the issues were simple. There were no distractions, no cities, no railroads, shops, cinemas, markets, farms, children or women. There was no fifth column, and there were no politics. We never saw money or crowds or animals or hills and valleys. We saw the arching sky and the flat desert stretching away on every side. Consequently the small incident (as distinct from the set-piece battle) achieved a significance it would never have had in Europe or the tropics, and we saw it clearly, we saw all round it, we knew its beginning and its effect. Certainty of detail like this seldom falls to the journalist. He works at such speed he has no time for a methodical checking of his facts and so he has to hedge, to qualify, to suggest rather than to state a fact. In the desert it was much easier. We could state a thing boldly because we saw it in isolation, and most events other than the actual battles came as clearly before our eyes as a single ship at sea. Moreover our own lives were simple.

The desert had an antiseptic effect upon nearly everyone who went there in the war. That is to say it destroyed most of the small indulgences and even the vices that eat like parasites into our lives in normal times. In this immense untenanted space it was nearly impossible to commit any of the deadly sins; the food was appalling (mostly bully beef and biscuit), liquor virtually non-existent, and so the glutton inside oneself withered away. In the complete absence of women, even of pornographic books, advertisements and entertainments, there was no stimulus to sexual desire except that which was self-induced by dreams and secret memories; and even the echoes of such vicarious, unanswered lust tended to grow faint after a time. It was absurd to be avaricious, envious or jealous where no one had any possessions or privileges to speak of, and the desert by its very nature compelled the slothful man to bestir himself in order to remain alive. Then, too, the fear of death and wounding in this distant place was a mighty destroyer of pride. This enforced monasticism might, of course, in itself have been more deadly, more stultifying, than any sin, had not the desert provided its own distractions and its own bizarre rewards.

Later on when there were a million soldiers on the Egyptian front a plague of flies descended on us, and the sandstorms became unbearable because the ground was cut up into fine dust by so many tanks and trucks. A stale and desolate air hung about the great dumps of provisions and the army workshops. But during this early period which I am now describing the desert was as fresh and sparkling as the slopes of a mountain after a heavy fall of snow. The wheels of our car cut into sand that had never been trodden upon, and often, towards midday, the horizon quivered in a watery haze and mirages grew up into the air, turreted medieval cities floating on a lake, mysterious forests trailing grey and purple mists, and groups of bedouin in their robes advancing upon us upside down. Then, in the evening, when the terrible, blasting, stultifying heat of the sun began to subside at last, we returned to our camp on the coast and ran naked across white sand beaches into the transparent sea. Lying on one's back, feeling the clotted dust washing away from one's ears, eyes and throat, one saw the cliffs turn scarlet in the sunset light, and presently we were once again under the protective cover of the night.

The darkness was our deliverance. Each morning there was an hour of grace when the sky was filled with a cool apple-green light, but then the sun lifted its mad glaring eye over the horizon and the sense of dread returned. The first hours of the morning were the worst because we were now uncovered to the sight of the enemy and we had so long to wait for the next holiday of the night.

The nights were cold. One spread out one's camp bed on the open sand with a waterproof sheet on top, and in the morning the hollows of the sheet were filled with dew. No light could be shown in the darkness, and so we went to bed at dusk, and that was the moment when, gazing up at stars that were twice as bright as any that are ever seen in Europe, Alex and I resumed that effortless, absorbing conversation that is only made possible by a long skein of shared experiences.

We talked at first of the things we had done that day, and of how we thought the front would develop and of where we should go on the morrow. We talked of our writing and of how to improve it, and finally we talked about ourselves. I was just thirty, Alex a year older, and neither of us had been very happy as adolescents or successful as young men. But now, together, we were triumphant. Our two camp beds sailed out into space and time and we were exactly poised and at peace. There we sat like birds in the wilderness, we were free, and there seemed at last in this murmured exchange of ideas to be an explanation for the mystery of simply being alive. To speak the dream—that was the thing: the backward dream of all that had already happened and the forward dream of what we hoped would be; and this was not difficult because we were, in fact, perched on a kind of mental frontier; our old lives had come to an abrupt stop with the war and with our arrival here in the desert, and no one could say what was going to happen to us after the war was over.

When at length we went to sleep it was because we had nothing more to say that night, we were emptied for the moment of every thought we had and only a pleasant drowsy euphoria remained.

Gibraltar

Looking back, I suppose that the first time I could ever call myself a foreign correspondent was the time I went to Gibraltar in 1937 for the *Daily Express*. It was a minor beginning. With all the official restrictions the difficulty of obtaining news for my paper was very great; the war in Spain might have been a thousand miles away for all the information we were able to get about it in Gibraltar, and the British officials were under orders not to communicate with the press in case anything of an embarrassing nature should leak out and prejudice the garrison's neutrality. The Chief Secretary was quite a pleasant fellow, but he told me flatly when I called upon him that he would expel me from the Rock if I published anything which he considered subversive. There was no censorship of course, he said—nothing like that. I just had to be careful.

Thus I was reduced to hanging about the bars in the main streets, to questioning the crews of the incoming merchant ships, and to scanning the Straits and the Spanish mainland with my binoculars. Cable after cable came in from the foreign editor asking me for information about what was going on and I simply did not know. It was an additional irritation that these cables took hours to reach me because they were first passed to any of the garrison officials who might be interested.

Within a week I had visited all the bars and restaurants and cinemas on the Rock. Within ten days I had played on all the tennis courts and bathed from all the beaches. Within a month I knew by sight all the leading people in the town, had eaten every variety of food and had heard the full uninspiring range of conversation which usually revolved around rates of government pay and the habits of Spanish servants. Thereafter all these things simply repeated themselves over and over again until the mind reeled with boredom and life retreated into an aimless and listless routine.

From my balcony at the Rock Hotel I looked across the blue water of the straits to the coast of Africa, fourteen miles away. Behind the hotel grey limestone rock covered with scrub rose up to a jagged outline against the pale, clear sky, and over to the west lay the mainland of Spain itself, a mysterious and forbidden territory since it was impossible to obtain a Spanish visa.

Down below on the edge of the sea the hot and ugly little town huddled around the dockyards and the barracks, which were also forbidden to civilians like myself. Warships and merchant vessels kept passing in and out of the harbour, and in the evening, when sailors in white uniforms filled the narrow streets of the town, gusts of identical flamenco music rose up from a thousand radios. Each day the sun shone brightly and it was always warm enough to swim.

The British officers almost to a man were supporters of General Franco; for them he represented law and order, the survival of decency over the mob; the Spanish navy had gone over to the General's side and that was sufficient proof of his worthiness. Among the rest of the Gibraltese there was a variety of opinion. The dockyard workers were notoriously 'red', even though La Linea was now under Franco's control, and in Gibraltar they spoke freely about their hatred of the new regime in Andalusia. Many of the minor British were temperamentally opposed to the idea of dictatorship, and they kept alive in Gibraltar a confused sort of liberalism, which gathered fuel from the news of the Fascist atrocities in Spain.

But all this was secondary. However vociferously they talked, very few people in Gibraltar really felt deeply about the civil war or the issues that were being decided there. Their fundamental desire was to keep out, and to continue with their own peaceful lives.

Each morning I sat down in the same chair in the same cafe and read the Gibraltar *Gazette* over a cup of coffee. The same habitués dropped in.

'Hot enough for you?'

'It certainly is.'

'It looks like another levanter.'

'Feels like it anyway.'

The levanter was an African wind that brought in a sea mist from the straits. It was so thick that it blotted out the crest of the Rock. The sun vanished but the heat was redoubled; by mid-afternoon the air was flat, lifeless and hardly breathable. People walked by like ghosts with pale and sweating faces, and at the least irritation one complained like a petulant child. It was on these days that the guns on the upper Rock often engaged in practice shooting into the Mediterranean. If one opened one's windows the glass remained intact, but nothing could prevent those shattering explosions from hitting the head with the effect of a hammer; nor was any aspirin proof against the ensuing headache.

Occasionally one escaped for a day or two across the straits to Tangier, which was our Paris in the Mediterranean. It contained casinos and night-clubs, bistros with bearable food, brothels and sellers of drugs and pornographic books. I returned from my weekends in Tangier penniless, tired and disillusioned. One stepped ashore at Gibraltar like an exhausted tripper after a hard day on Hampstead Heath, and the routine closed in again.

And then these dog-days abruptly came to an end. One evening the German battleship *Deutschland* steamed slowly into Gibraltar harbour. She came in under the shadow of the Rock just as it was getting dark, but it was still light enough for those who were watching on the

3*

shore to see that almost the entire after-deck was covered with lines of coffins, and each coffin was draped with the Nazi flag—the crooked cross on the red ground. Sentries with bowed heads stood among the dead.

The *Deutschland* had been sheltering off Iviza in the Balearic Islands, ostensibly doing duty as one of the warships which France, Britain and Germany had posted around the coasts of Spain with the object of preventing supplies or men being sent in to either of the belligerents in the civil war. She had a perfect right to cruise round the Balearics; that was her station.

Both Italy and Germany of course were far from being neutral in the Spanish war: Mussolini was already sending great quantities of arms and men to the help of General Franco and Hitler was preparing to follow suit. It was even said that ships like the *Deutschland* were shining their searchlights into the sky at night to guide the Italian bombers on their way to attack the Republican cities of Valencia and Barcelona, and that the German sailors turned a blind eye to the Italian submarines which were then sinking neutral vessels almost every other week in the Mediterranean. The whole scheme of the non-intervention patrol was in fact a cynical farce and could never be made to work because neither Italy nor Germany could be persuaded to honour it.

All this was true enough (just as it was also true that France was not seriously impeding the flow of left-wing volunteers across the Pyrenees into Barcelona); but the fact remained that the *Deutschland* was fulfilling her legal duty in the Balearics, and ought not to have been attacked. Yet she was attacked and very seriously.

A Spanish Republican pilot flew out from the Catalonian seaboard, and whether or not he mistook the *Deutschland* for some other vessel is perhaps beside the point; he deliberately took aim and with exceptional skill dropped his bombs into the middle of the ship. They penetrated the

armoured deck and burst with immense violence in one of
the ward-rooms where, just at that moment, a number of
officers were eating a meal. And now the *Deutschland* had
steamed into Gibraltar to land her dead and wounded.

Quite apart from those lines of coffins on the after-deck
it was apparent that something was wrong in the ship
directly she came alongside. I could see little damage
beyond the scalding of the grey paint on her sides, but
there was an air of suppressed tension among the crew,
something almost bordering on hysteria. The sailors who
ran to lower the gang-plank fumbled with the ropes and
finally dropped the unwieldy thing with a clatter on the
wharf. Twice more they hauled it up and dropped it again
before it was made secure at last. Other sailors who had
gone off to carry the coffins to the shore stumbled about
the deck in a confused and awkward way, bumping into
one another, picking up their burdens and irresolutely
dumping them again, apparently unable to understand their
orders. The remainder of the German crew was drawn up
in a series of long ceremonial ranks along the decks facing
the shore and they too were restless despite the wooden
and expressionless appearance of their faces. More and
more officers kept hurrying aft to try and obtain some order
out of the confusion around the gang-plank. Presently
stretcher-bearers began to appear on deck with the
wounded.

All this time in the gathering darkness groups of British
officers and sailors who had been suddenly called from their
evening meal were eyeing the strange scene from the
wharf. They stood in their white summer uniforms not ten
yards away from the side of the *Deutschland* and this was
the first time they had seen the famous ship which had been
built with so much secrecy, or the men whom one day they
would have to fight. It was, moreover, their first real
vision of war, of the power and the harm of high explosive.
The Rock of Gibraltar reared up behind us like the wall of

a chasm, dark at the top where the guns were hidden, sprinkled with the lights of the town at the base, and the sea was unusually calm all the way across the Straits to Africa.

No word was exchanged between the ship and the shore until at last the first wounded were brought down the gang-plank, and British ambulances with open doors came backing up to the water's edge to receive them. Two young German officers hastily conferred with the British, and now a bright light was hoisted up above the wharf so that we could all see one another very clearly.

When the first ambulances drove away and there were still many wounded to come off, a sudden commotion occurred among the German ratings drawn up on the decks. First one or two, then a dozen, then whole parties of a score or more, broke their ranks and vaulted over the side of the ship on to the wharf. No order had been given them; they moved apparently out of a blind and over-powering desire to get out of that ship with its dead and put their feet on solid land again. Soon there was a white waterfall of human bodies pouring off the deck on to the land, and although the German officers shouted harshly to the men to keep their ranks, the movement still went on.

The sailors were extraordinarily young; the majority were hardly more than boys, and in their blue eyes and taut pink faces there was an expression of spontaneous relief, of panic subsiding nervously and erratically, but ready to break out again at any moment. They took no notice of the shouted orders from the deck. They ran to the dockside buildings and relieved themselves in the darkness there.

That night several more German sailors died in hospital, and there was a great coming and going on the Rock. Volunteer nurses were hastily bundled into uniform and an urgent radio call was put through to London for more of them to be flown out. There were conferences with the

Bishop and the authorities at the cemetery where the dead Germans were to be buried in a common grave. The military and the police were called on to assist in arranging for the *Deutschland*'s crew to march through the town on the morrow with their dead. Hitler himself, we were told, was demanding news of the death-roll, and between the *Deutschland* and Germany, between the Governor and London, between the foreign consuls and their governments, the communications were in a ferment.

It was a moment of ghoulish release and I enjoyed every minute of it. Now at last the lifeless routine was broken, and I had a story to write at last. It was perfectly obvious that some sort of drastic aftermath would follow and that night on the Rock we were all waiting to see what Hitler would do. Next morning the *Deutschland*'s crew marched heavily and slowly through the Gibraltar streets with their dead comrades. One by one the coffins in their Nazi flags were lowered into the great grave which Spanish workmen had excavated during the night; it lay on the one flat patch of ground at the northern extremity of the Rock.

While this was going on Hitler found a thing to do. He sent a second battleship, the *Von Spee*, to the little republican town of Almeria, which lay to the east of Gibraltar, about 150 miles along the coast. And there, in the early morning, without warning of any kind, the *Von Spee* opened fire upon the inhabitants. The ship stood close into the shore with an attendant destroyer and shelled the town methodically for half an hour; then it turned and sailed away.

The shelling of Almeria was, in its small way, a more startling thing for the local people than the explosion of the first atomic bomb at Hiroshima. The Japanese at least knew that they were in a war and that bombing was to be expected at any time. The peasants and the fishermen of Almeria had no such preparation. As yet they had been untouched by the fighting which had passed through the

larger cities of Spain. That lazy backwater life of southern
Andalusia had simply continued as it had done for centuries, and except for a handful of alert officials the issues
of the civil war had never succeeded in making a strong
appeal to the inhabitants one way or the other. Many of
them could neither read nor write. They had never heard
of the German battleship *Deutschland* and still less did they
know anything of how she had been bombed from the air
at Iviza. They were engaged in their usual tasks on this
early summer morning: the women were shaking out their
mats and bedding at their doorways, the donkeys were
bringing in sacks of vegetables to the market square, and
on the beach the fishermen were mending their nets. It
was seven o'clock and there was a promise of another hot
day. A light sea mist was lifting from the shore.

Then, suddenly, out of nowhere, six-inch shells began to
explode in the streets. And while the houses were ripped
about, spilling their furniture out of doors, and craters
opened by magic in the roadways, many terrified animals
went screaming through the market place. Men and women
stood dumbly for a moment, not knowing where to go or
what to do. But then, when the explosions repeated themselves, they too joined in the stampede, some flinging
themselves into their houses to hide, others running blindly
for the open countryside, others again snatching up their
children and making for the nearest church. Some in their
terror and confusion thought that this was an earthquake;
others believed that it was a thunderbolt sent by God and
sank to their knees to pray. Fires started up and in every
direction uprooted trees and lumps of masonry were hurt-
ling through the air. A priest attempted to peal the church
bells, but their call was scarcely heard above the stupendous noise of the bursting shells and the screams and the
cries of the wounded who were now calling for help from
almost every part of the town. Even when the bombard-
ment stopped at last it was by no means apparent to the

people that the worst was over because the town was enveloped with the smoke of the fires and the noise of falling timbers and the general uproar created by those who were hysterical with fright or shock or the sight of blood.

In this way Hitler revenged himself for the bombs that fell upon his battleship *Deutschland*. Except for the fact that the people he attacked had nothing to do with the *Deutschland* it was an ample revenge, for he took many more lives than those that had been lost in the ship.

I happen to know about the shelling because I was posted off to Almeria by my paper as soon as the news came through. It is true that I took a week to get there on a tramp ship, the only means of travel available, but the debris of the town was still an appalling thing to see and the incidents of that fatal morning were of course very fresh in the people's minds. Many of them still thought that the shelling was a natural phenomenon; it was not conceivable that human beings could behave so savagely as this.

No Pasaran

With the *Deutschland* incident the Spanish war made a great stride towards us—it became, in a sense, everybody's war—and it was certainly brought a great deal nearer to me. I was sent off to the Mediterranean to try and find out just how and by whom the ships bringing supplies into Barcelona and Valencia were being sunk. It was an impossible assignment to fulfil, but I embarked upon it with gusto since it enabled me to escape from Gibraltar. I had had six months on the Rock and that was quite enough.

An Italian passenger liner took me as far as Algiers; I then transhipped to a German freighter which sailed for Turkey, where I hoped to get aboard one of the oil-tankers coming down into the Mediterranean from Russia. Now at last I felt I was getting into the war. What actually happened was that I was catapulted into the world of Eric Ambler and Graham Greene.

I came ashore at Istanbul without a single coherent idea of what I was to do next. At the Tokatlian Hotel they gave me a narrow room without a bath and the porter was not helpful. 'Do you want a guide?' he said. 'Want to see the Blue Mosque?'

I wandered out into the streets again and stood for a while gazing at the statue of Kemal Ataturk. He was carved boldly in stone and he was wearing a dinner-jacket and turned-up cuffs on the bottom of his trousers. Camels and mules and street vendors with their handcarts passed by, covering the statue's elegant legs with dust. Somehow, I thought, I must discover the technique of the high-powered foreign correspondent. He would not stand here,

in the midday heat, with his hands in his pockets staring at
a statue of Kemal Ataturk. He would be dining at embassies, telephoning Cabinet Ministers, sending off long
political cables, perhaps interviewing Kemal Ataturk himself. But how did one begin? Suppose you had no local
money, spoke no word of Turkish, knew no one, had never
set foot in Istanbul before, and suppose you felt slightly
sick in the stomach because the ground kept heaving up
and down, how did you penetrate that magic world?

Within an hour I found out. I had borrowed five
Turkish pounds from the porter at the Tokatlian and was
sitting at a café, longing for the clean safe berth in which I
had travelled from Gibraltar, when I was approached by a
plump little man in a crumpled linen suit. He asked me for
a light, we started to talk, I told him I was a journalist in
Istanbul on a job and it turned out that—strangely enough
—he was a journalist himself. He whisked a card out of his
breast pocket. 'Andropoulos. Special correspondent of the
Agence Havas in Istanbul.' Plainly he was neither French
nor Turkish nor Greek, though possibly a mixture of all
three; but then I could scarcely have cared less if he had
been a Samoan islander. M. Andropoulos was my entrée
into the world of cabinet ministers and embassies. In a
moment he was telling me the intimate news of Istanbul.

It seemed that apart from the Russian government ship-
ments there were several companies engaged in the
enterprise of breaking the blockade on Spain, and their
methods were much the same. Decrepit tramps and
tankers were bought up for a song, and whether or not
they had a Lloyd's certificate made little difference. The
Spanish government was paying so well that a single cargo
would cover the cost of the ship; and if a ship made only
two successful voyages before she got sunk then it was still
good business. The crews of these ships were the toughest
characters from the Middle East docks, men made
desperate by poverty or drink or crime or some other

quarrel with society, men who were willing for double or triple rates of pay to undertake the unusual risks of the passage through the Sicilian Narrows to Valencia and Barcelona. Not all, of course, were like this, but that was the average.

Could I get a berth on one of these ships? But naturally, said M. Andropoulos, it could be arranged. It was a secret and difficult business but he would put me in touch with a friend of his, a white Russian who was the agent for a group of ships, a man in a very big way of business. 'I should not bother very much about his name,' he said; 'you may call him Mr Brandt.'

That same evening, at seven o'clock, M. Andropoulos called for me in a very large American car with a chauffeur and drove me to the southern side of the town.

Mr Brandt was waiting in the garden. He sat in a wicker chair, an albino, a large fleshy man with an enormous head which gave him a certain toad-like appearance, all pink and white. He wore a crumpled grey palm beach suit, and as we talked flapped a purple fly-whisk languidly in the air. We spoke through an interpreter, and Mr Brandt was in no hurry whatever. We drank coffee out of little eggshell cups half filled with coffee grounds. We deplored the weather. We ate the little round cakes made of coconut and sugar. We exclaimed over the splendours of the Blue Mosque and the evening light across the Golden Horn. We sipped at our glasses of iced water.

'There are three sources of water in Constantinople and the moment he puts a glass to his lips an expert will tell you from what spring that particular water was drawn,' said Mr Brandt. He waited with elaborate attention while each of his sentences was translated. 'If you go into the bazaar you will find men selling all three varieties. They carry the water in a goatskin on their backs and they offer it in little silver glasses. Very often they will make no charge but simply ask you to pray for the soul of Ibrahim so and so. This simply means that Ibrahim has recently died, and as a last gesture his relatives have paid the water-seller to supply some fifty or perhaps a hundred free glasses to passers-by in the street, so that they will inter-cede for his soul. It is one of the most charming customs in the old quarter.'

Plainly Mr Brandt was going through a long and devious process of sounding me out. He watched me care-fully while the interpreter spoke and listened closely to my responses. A gross and hay-coloured Persian cat stalked into the garden and heaved itself on to his lap, and he sat there softly stroking it with his hand and flapping his ivory-handled fly-whisk, a modern pasha giving an audience.

We passed on to a discussion of Leander's Tower and the swimming of the Hellespont by Lord Birkenhead, Lord Byron and others. There was some pun about swimming and the English peerage with which the inter-preter was grappling doubtfully, when suddenly Brandt asked: 'Why do you wish to sail to Spain?'

'I am the representative of an important group of English newspapers,' I said.

'So it is what you call a good story, then?'

'Yes, it is.'

'But suppose you see nothing?'

'Then I shall write nothing.'

'You have no other interest in this voyage, then? I mean it will be very uncomfortable.'

'It's my job,' I said, and then thinking over what he had just said I added: 'I'm not an agent or a spy if that's what you are thinking.'

'My dear sir!' He raised both flabby hands in the air and waved them deprecatingly. 'What a droll suggestion.' We both laughed merrily. A moment later he had steered the conversation back to San Sophia and the relics of the Ottoman Empire.

Two days later I got a message from Mr Brandt. A ship had arrived from Odessa and would be leaving at ten o'clock the next night for Valencia. She was an oil tanker called the *Tinos*. I was to be signed on as a supercargo and the captain would accommodate me in his own cabin.

*

The *Tinos* looked like any other tanker as she lay off the mouth of the Golden Horn in the half light of the evening; a long flat splinter of a ship, painted dirty grey, her bridge well aft, and she was laden right down to her plimsoll line with eight thousand tons of Rumanian petrol. She flew the flag of the Panama Republic, and this was the only Panamanian thing about her, since the captain was Russian, the first mate Greek, the wireless operator Rumanian, and the rest of the crew were Slavs, Levantines, Turks, Armenians, Arabs and Cypriots. This much I learned from the Greek mate who came to meet me at the docks. He spoke a kind of doggerel English, and it was possible to follow the general drift of what he was saying. This was important for me as he turned out to be the only man on board who spoke more than a few words of English.

Around us now the lights of the city had come up, making long quivering yellow snakes across the water, and in the distance the domes of the mosques had the appearance of floating on a mist between the city and the sky. All the filth and ugliness of Istanbul had quietened; even the smells of the land died away, and except for the dipping of the oars the only sounds around us were the occasional frantic whistles of the ferry steamers. Every now and then a gobbet of phosphorus came out of the black sea on the blade of an oar and shimmered briefly for a second before it was churned back into the wake of the boat. Little by little the bulk of the *Tinos* grew larger before us and separated itself from the outlines of the other ships at anchor there; and already, as one does, I found myself identifying myself with her. This for the moment was my refuge and home.

The captain was waiting for me as I came up the side on a rope ladder. 'Me Stanovitch,' he said, or some such name, and led the way down to the saloon. The first view of him was not reassuring. He had a round, moonlike face, smooth and pink and almost jolly except for the two sly little sky-blue eyes which almost disappeared into his fat cheeks when he laughed. He was a very big man, and everything about him was big and round, his hands and thighs and his shoulders. He wore a dirty blue uniform and a cap with the badge of some extinct steamship line. Day and night he was followed about the ship by a Chinese-Russian steward named Boris, who looked as if he had dressed up for a minor part in ballet; black boots, baggy Turkish pantaloons and an unwashed smock caught round his waist with a greasy leather belt.

The saloon was hot beyond all bearing and even when we took off our coats it made little difference. Someone years ago had made an attempt at elegance in the captain's saloon. A crimson velvet cloth, heavily tasselled, lay across the table. The chairs and benches were stuffed with horse-hair and covered with strong black leather. Two or three plush cushions were scattered about and the sideboard was backed with a large mirror cut into a series of elaborate floral patterns. The room was lit by a pendant lamp which swung with the rocking of the ship. It was moored to the deck above with a heavy brass bracket fashioned into the shapes of flying angels.

All this intensive *decor* must have been a stimulating sight some thirty or forty years before when it was first put in; but now the mirror was discoloured, the horse-hair had burst through to the surface of the cracked leather seats, two of the brass angels had lost their wings, and the crimson cloth was marked with a solar system of

grease spots revolving around a particularly heavy blot at
the captain's end of the table. And over everything was
that stuffy, airless dreariness of a confined space which has
been used too long and too often by unwashed human
beings.

There was no sound of the ship getting under way, and
it became apparent that nothing whatever was being done
in that direction. It was also apparent that the captain was
very drunk. His round face gleamed and glistened under
the light, and his conversation was reduced to the one
word 'Drink'. We clashed glasses of vodka together over
the centre of the table and the liquor went down my throat
like fire. I rose unsteadily. 'Sleep,' I said, 'where do I
sleep?'

The captain got up with a wide and happy smile and
embraced me, and that huge sweating form closed over my
head like mud. Then he crooked his little finger, playfully
beckoning me to the door, and closed one of his sly little
eyes in a repulsive wink. I followed doubtfully through the
door.

The captain's cabin was a long rectangular affair
divided in two by a curtain. Just now the curtain was
drawn, revealing the captain's bunk, his dressing-table,
his voluminous coats hanging from brass pegs and a little
electric light burning at an ikon above his pillow. My bags
had been dumped in the outer compartment, and here there
was a second bunk made up for me. It stood some four feet
above the deck on top of a series of wooden lockers, and
the blessed air was rushing through a porthole by the
pillars. There was a curtain on a brass rail which could be
pulled along the outer edge of the bunk much in the same
way as in the old pullman cars in America.

'Schleep,' said the captain with an elegant wave of his
hand. He took a seat at his own end of the cabin and fixed
me with the benign but penetrating stare of the drunk. I
fumbled in a haze of alcohol with the straps of my bags,

feeling sick and gloomy. Undressing was a long and clumsy performance, and when I stood naked for a moment grappling with my pyjama trousers I could feel that un-blinking stare travelling over my body. 'Good night,' I said, and heaved myself on to the bunk. He got up and advanced to my end of the cabin. Then he reached out his hand and I grabbed it quickly and shook it. 'Good night,' I said, and pulled the curtain between us. Then there was silence in the cabin.

I knew he was still standing by the curtain. I yawned loudly and deliberately. 'Perhaps if I sleep a little,' I whispered. 'Perhaps if the porthole were a little wider. Perhaps if I talked to the Greek mate in the morning. Perhaps there is someone in this hell ship who would lead me to a little water.' My eyes felt as though they were moved on leaden weights like the china eyes of a child's doll, and still I could not keep them closed. The deck was only a few inches above my head, and I began to study one by one the little bubbles of paint that had come out in the heat. There was a faint starlight gleam reflected off the water, and occasionally in the distance the faint sound of the last ferries crossing to Scutari. If only the *Tinos* would get started.

The curtain slid back quite slowly and as soon as it began to move I knew I had been expecting this. It receded inch by inch until it was entirely folded back at the end of the bunk. I made no move. I lay on my back with my eyes almost closed and breathed heavily like a sleeper through my nose. I had no notion of what I was going to do but I could see him standing there, barely a yard away, looking down on to me, and I waited.

Presently he put out his hand. It was a hand that came up from the darkness below the edge of the bunk, and even when it reached out and the fingers closed round my thigh and began working upward I still did nothing because a kind of paralysis had taken hold of me. I lay rigid, either unable or unwilling to cry out, and incapable of moving. Then abruptly, as though someone had struck me in the face, as though an unendurably bright light had suddenly emerged, comet-like, out of nowhere and splashed itself in my eyes, I was seized by a spasm of frantic horror. I rolled over to the edge of the bunk, and as I rolled I struck downward as far as I could towards his belly. I felt the flesh sag in. I heard him fall back grunting, and the momentum of the blow carried me half out of the bunk so that my left foot came in contact with his chest and I kicked with all my strength.

The captain was probably not much more drunk than I was, and in normal circumstances could have demolished and overlaid me without exerting himself. But he was not possessed as I was by the power of hysterical fear, and he was not expecting the blow. He fell with a crash to the deck, with me on top of him. Then while I scrambled round the cabin looking for any sort of a weapon I saw with intense relief there was no fight in him at all. Great tears were welling out of his eyes, and he heaved himself up painfully, muttering in Russian, as he groped his way blindly and awkwardly through the cabin towards his bunk.

For a moment he stood swaying. Then he collapsed full-length on his blanket, and I found myself standing there with a seaboot in my hand and trembling badly. Once more he heaved himself up and peered drunkenly into his ikon; then down he went again, and presently through the darkness I could hear that he was asleep. I crept out of the door and up on to the deck, drinking in the coolness of the night, and waiting for my breathing to become regular again. Across the bay the lights of the city were gradually going out and the ferries had stopped for the night.

In the morning when I woke we were far down the Sea of Marmora. I was bewildered for a moment by the throbbing of the ship, the strange ceiling above, and the distempered hangover of my dreams mingling with the memory of what had actually happened on the night before; but at once, like the focusing of a camera, everything took its place, and I snatched back the curtain and looked out. There was no sign of the captain. I leaned back happily and watched the play of green and yellow light reflected from the water on to the white paint above me.

So this then was the Sea of Marmora, where the British submarines penetrated in the 1914 War, and presently we would be in the Dardanelles; on our right, Gallipoli, and on the left the ruins of the fabulous city of Troy. And behind Troy, Mount Ida. 'Listen, Mother Ida. Hearken ere I die.' Byron?

By daylight the *Tinos* was an unexpectedly trim ship. Burning oil herself and carrying no other cargo but oil there was no litter on her broad iron decks, nothing in fact to see there but the cocks above each tank, a lifeboat or two and the big rubber hoses for pumping out the cargo at our destination. The oil tanks lay forward of the bridge and on the bridge alone smoking was permitted. A long raised catwalk ran from the bridge to the men's quarters in the foc'sle.

It was dead calm in this landlocked sea, and the warm water flopped back from the bows like blue jelly being sliced open with a knife. All around us there was a strong white light shining from the sea, and a heat haze blocked the view of the shore. It was going to be another roasting day; already one could feel the heat of the iron decks coming through the soles of one's shoes.

I found the Greek mate alone on the bridge. There was not much to do, he said. 'We cannot use the radio once we are in the central Mediterranean for fear of attracting attention. There are eight thousand tons of petrol on board. One bomb and the whole thing goes sky high.'

'Do you think we will be attacked?'

'I don't know. Nothing can happen till we get near

Malta anyway. It's when we turn north and try to make a
dash past the Balearics to get into Valencia inside twenty-
four hours—that's the dangerous bit.'

But on the whole he was fatalistic. The ship was solid
and secure enough under our feet in the Turkish sunshine.

The *Tinos* was an eight-knot ship, or rather that was the
economical speed at which they sailed her, and so it was
not until late afternoon when the heat haze lifted that the
shores of the Sea of Marmora began to converge in upon
us as we approached the mouth of the Dardanelles. The
captain appeared at lunch, grumpy and non-committal. At
six in the evening we ate again, and then under the starlight I watched the banks of the Dardanelles slipping by.

Already I was adjusting myself to the routine of the
ship; the hours of the watches, the times of the meals, the
coming and going of the crew—all those things which
were going to be repeated precisely hour by hour and day
by day until the end of the journey. At first this balanced,
this unvarying routine, appeared to be entirely fixed and
monotonous. But later I began to detect many little
nuances and disturbances of the rhythm. Sometimes it
would be no more than a look on a man's face, or a tone of
voice or the arrival of a sailor on the bridge at an unusual
time, and one knew at once that some unplanned under-
current had been let loose, that this was the signal of
intense hatreds or jealousies or rivalries that were barely
under control. It was as though one were sitting in an
aeroplane whose motors at first appeared to beat on the
one unchanging note. But later, when the ear became
attuned, the slightest variation in the pitch struck the
mind like a thunderclap. And on the *Tinos*, every move,
every spoken word had a sharpened meaning because soon
we would be in danger and everything was said and done in
apprehension of that fact. The eight thousand tons of
petrol created a sort of mental shadow that followed one's
thoughts wherever they went.

The captain made no further effort to molest me, but he remained a menace. Each night when I came to undress I found him sitting there in the cabin, watching. He did no more than this; just sat and watched. During this short period his surliness vanished, he chuckled and made grimaces and tried to talk English. And then when I was in my bunk he slowly undressed himself and got into a large white nightshirt. For a moment he knelt and prayed before his icon and finally he fell heavily into bed and was immediately asleep. He lay flat on his back, his pink cheeks puffing in and out, his great hands clasped across his stomach. When I woke in the morning he was always gone.

Once in the night I found him standing over me, silently peering through the curtain in the darkness. It sounded as though he was weeping; but he made no other move and presently he went back to his own end of the cabin. On another occasion when I came unexpectedly into the cabin during the morning I found him rummaging through my underclothes. He picked up a pair of blue silk underpants and waved them at me chuckling and nodding; then abruptly he turned round and went out.

He ruled the ship like a tyrant, which was probably the only way to rule it, since one thing and one thing only had brought these thirty or forty men together, and that was money. Then too he was an efficient sailor and one had the feeling that if we were going into danger he would remain calm and take accurate decisions. He was a bully but not a coward. I had very little contact with the crew, partly because we had no common language and partly because it was generally supposed that I had been brought on board to satisfy the captain's unnatural lusts. No matter how angry I felt there was no way of scotching his libel.

The *Tinos* slid through a calm and oily sea. We emerged from the mouth of the Dardanelles and sailed just west of south past Lemnos and Mytilene and there was never so much as a breeze to disturb the Aegean. The early summer sun came up hot and red each morning and continued all through the cloudless day until that moment when it was extinguished with a green flash on the western horizon. Occasionally other ships went by, occasionally the crest of some Greek island shot up briefly and beautifully in the distance, but that was all; there was no other incident.

Each morning after breakfast I trod my measured number of paces along the catwalk from the bridge to the foc'sle and back again. From eleven till noon I talked to the mate on the bridge and after lunch I slept. Then again the walk round the ship, pausing at my favourite places, the chicken-coop where four withered hens crouched listlessly on the hot iron deck, the wheelhouse, the portside lifeboat, the stern where the *Tinos* shuddered and wriggled like a dog shaking his tail and the wake came frothing up to the surface in streams of blue white bubbles. Finally dinner and bed. Twice I wrote brief newspaper messages and the radio operator painfully tapped out the English phrases on his radio transmitter to the nearest shore station, Athens at first, then Taranto. But there was really nothing to say. Crete slipped away to the south, and we sailed on through the velvet sea towards Malta.

On the sixth morning I looked out of my port-hole and beheld a marvellous sight. The British battle-cruiser *Hood* was sailing abreast of us, not three miles away, and she was followed, like ducklings clustered round their mother, by half a dozen merchant ships, all steaming westward like ourselves. The *Hood* at that time was the biggest warship at sea, and she was also by some accident or genius of design the most beautiful. She gave no impression of dead weight or immensity; she was shaped in the lines of a yacht and if she was strong then it was graceful strength. The lean grey bows broke the water with a peculiar lightness of movement, as though she was being driven by the breeze.

Plainly our eight thousand tons of petrol was a great deal safer so long as the *Hood* was there, and I could feel the *Tinos* increasing her speed and changing direction in order to join the convoy. We were not yet in the danger zone, but Sicily lay just to the north and Pantelleria, reputedly an Italian submarine base, was directly ahead. It was believed that the aircraft and ships which were attacking merchantmen in the Mediterranean at that time were operating much further to the West, from the Balearic Islands, but there was no assurance that Mussolini might not also be sending out raiders from Italian territory. And so the *Hood* was a friendly sight. We stayed with her all day, but then towards evening she suddenly increased her speed to fifteen knots and effortlessly pulled away to the horizon just at the moment when the sun was going down. The chief engineer who was sharing my usual evening watch shook his head sadly and went below.

On the seventh morning we were alone again at sea. The other freighters had scattered in the night, and now by herself the *Tinos* sailed up to the Tunisian coast. Cape Bon came up, a great rose-coloured cliff across the calm water, and as we sailed inside the three-mile limit everybody's spirits rose. Even if we were attacked here it was no great distance to swim to the shore. And as we crept along the coast, hour by hour, on the eighth and ninth days, past Bone and Phillipeville and Djelli, and at night the friendly lights shone from the shore, a sense of lassitude and security filled the mind, and it seemed a monstrous improbability that any danger should come out of the sea, that ships should be bombed and sunk, that men should want to murder one another. I sent off a message to the *Express* saying all was well.

What we wanted now was a storm, any sort of a storm to hide us at that critical moment when we must turn north

from the north African coast and run through the dangerous open sea for Valencia. But still the sun shone on, and
still the glass was high.

Then on the tenth day, when we were passing Algiers,
for the first time a bank of white clouds climbed lazily into
the western sky and there was the faintest perceptible
ripple on the glassy water. By evening the glass was falling, the Atlas mountains on the shore were blurred in
mist, and the whole horizon was overcast. We were now
approaching Oran. The *Tinos* had been taken far out of her
course so that she would have the protection of French
territorial waters until the last possible moment; but at
some point of the night we must turn north and face the
menace of the Balearics.

The storm hit us at nine o'clock. It began with a gentle
rocking as I sat reading beneath the wingless brass angels
in the saloon, and presently the lamp started to sway back
and forth in little jerks. For the first time since we had left
Istanbul a sharp cool draught of air came down the
ventilator into that solid atmosphere of stale grease and
kitchen smells. By the time I reached the bridge the whole
ship was full of the noise of sighing and straining woodwork, and the crew were running about the deck and along
the catwalk with a speed I had never seen before. Through
his megaphone the captain was bellowing orders. Some of
the men had gone to the lifeboats and in a confusion of
shouting and cursing were lowering them over the sides.

'Good God,' I shouted in panic to the mate, 'are we
sinking?'

He heaved his shoulders impatiently. 'We turn north,'
he said. 'Plenty bombs . . . get boats ready.'

Abashed but relieved, I saw that the African coast was
already out of sight, and now we were in the open sea. All
around us little black waves, flecked with white, were
running past in front of the wind. They hit the *Tinos*
broadside on with a series of angry flops and thuds and

then cascaded back like rain into the racing water. It was as if we were crossing a tremendous river which had suddenly broken into flood. Every now and then a specially big wave thumped against the ship's side, and she shied away like a startled horse, heeling over to starboard, protesting as she went. I shivered on the bridge. All that concentrated heat from the iron decks had vanished, and the clean cold wind was rushing into every cranny of the ship, routing out the stale air and all the congested human smells we had brought from the Middle East. The sky was not yet entirely overcast. At several places where the flying clouds wore thin great rifts opened up, and looking through into the limpid cobalt space beyond we could see the new moon lying on its back, serene and yellow. For a minute or two it played a sickly light on the surface of the sea and the tossing bows of the *Tinos*, and then the clouds rushed across again, blotting it out with the rapidity and the completeness of a camera shutter.

Among the crew there was a buoyancy and cheerfulness such as you might have had in the old days in a sailing ship which had been becalmed in a tropical sea. One imagines that the sails hang limp, the meat turns rotten, and as each airless night and hopeless day goes by all the repressed hatreds of the crew start festering in open quarrels. Then suddenly the fresh wind comes up and fills the sails, and everything which before was stale and hopeless is swept away and forgotten in the new movement of the ship.

The issues in the *Tinos* were perhaps more complicated than this, but it was the same kind of feeling. Everyone had dreaded this last stage of the journey when a submarine might strike at us in the moonlight, or an aircraft so easily pick us out as we lay exposed and helpless on a sunny sea. But now we were suddenly hidden by this providential storm, and if only it would continue on the morrow we might get through to Valencia unmolested. Then too on a lower key of feeling there was all that stimulus of coming out of the heat into the cool, of filling the lungs with fresh salt air at last, of escaping from the monotony of a sea that had been too calm for too long.

When I went below at eleven o'clock the glass was still falling and the wind if anything was still sharper than before. My porthole was closed but the cabin was much cooler than before, and I pulled up a blanket and lay on the bunk listening to the unusual sounds. Thump. Thump. Thump-thump. That was two small waves followed by a big one. It was pleasant to lie here safe and hear them hitting the side of the ship, just half an inch away. Directly behind my head and again farther down the cabin near the captain's bunk the wooden partitions were grating against one another, and they emitted two squeaks, a high one and a low one, with every roll of the ship. SQUEAK. Squeak. SQUEAK. Squeak. Thump. Thump. Thump.

I woke with a start in the morning. An extra heavy wave had hit the ship, and now there was a pandemonium of noises in the cabin. The squeaks in the woodwork had multiplied themselves a dozen times, and the deck of the cabin was a litter of brushes, tin mugs, shoes, books, shaving things and odd bits of clothing. My suitcases had skidded across the cabin in the night and overturned against the lockers. It was difficult to stand upright, let alone clear up the mess. But presently one adjusted oneself to the motion and I shaved well enough with cold water, making swipes at my face when the *Tinos* was in the middle of her roll. They had told me that petrol was a heavy and an excellent cargo in rough weather, but this now seemed to be an exaggeration. There were times when the ship shook herself from end to end like a terrier coming out of the water and then, before you could recover your balance, she seemed to be sliding headlong down the side of a steep wall.

I went directly on to the bridge. It was difficult to recognize either the *Tinos* or the sea. The accustomed world of yellow sunshine and blue water had vanished entirely; everything had turned to grey. A heavy grey rain flew almost horizontally across the ship, and it hit the waves with such force that they were pockmarked with a million little splashes; and the waves themselves had mounted up into furious grey mountains, forever collapsing and renewing themselves out to the jagged horizon, where there was no break in the forbidding sky, nothing but a torrent of racing grey-black clouds which almost touched the sea. There was a screeching, maniacal quality in the wind; it tore and tore at every obstacle as though it would pluck it out of existence, as though it would pluck out your eyes.

The *Tinos* with her eight knots and her eight thousand tons of petrol plunged into this tumult like a canoe in a cataract. It seemed as if she had no will of her own any more, but was simply suffering anything that might happen to her. All that flat expanse of deck from the bridge to the foc'sle was under a continuous stream of rushing water, so that the bridge and foc'sle appeared to be parts of two different ships having no connection with each other. When she rolled to starboard the sea poured off her in a long even waterfall until the next wave came up to meet the deck; and then, just when you were expecting to see the decks clear at last, she scooped up another great slice of the ocean and sent it careering back to the port side with a head of water four or five feet deep. Here, beneath the lifeboats, it was caught by the full force of the westerly wind and flung up as high and higher than the bridge in immense and frightening cascades of grey spray.

As I struggled up to the bridge one particularly malignant gust tore the last remaining chicken out of its wire coop. It squawked and flapped its wings absurdly for a moment as it was carried up towards the mast, and then it vanished in the rain.

The captain and the mate were standing together on the
4

bridge in their unfamiliar oilskins, holding on to the railing with both hands and doing nothing very much as far as I could see except endure the storm and wait for something better or worse to happen. They stared out at the surrounding wilderness of water with that set expression of men who have become fixed in the attitude of waiting, so that the mere act of waiting had become an end in itself, a test of endurance, a kind of rational defiance against the uncontrollable fury of the sea.

I began to have a grudging respect for the captain simply because of his standing there, accepting, as it were, responsibility for the storm and anything that it might do to the ship. No hot food had been cooked since daybreak, and all around us the sailors were slopping about with haggard and miserable faces. Already one man had broken his arm and half a dozen accidents had happened in the night. We carried no doctor, and the mate had been down to the foc'sle doing what he could with the first-aid kit.

The radio operator, yellow with sea-sickness, crouched over his silent radio in the cabin, and when I passed by he looked up with dog-like misery and turned away again. In the whole ship there was not a dry comfortable place where one could shut out the storm.

All that day the wind and rain kept beating on us from the west. At sunset there was a brief flicker of red and orange light through the clouds, and then everything was turned to utter blackness. No lights were allowed to show from the ship, and as one staggered about, lifebelt in hand, one's imagination leapt in to take the place of one's eyes, and the violence of the storm became magnified beyond all reason.

Everyone except the captain had long since forgotten Franco's bombers and submarines; they belonged to a man-made and predictable world and one could take certain dispositions against them. But this storm, like an earthquake or a volcanic explosion, was beyond any human control, and there could be no telling if it would become worse or how long it would continue. There was nothing to do but wait.

I got down on my bunk without undressing. I had a raging headache from the constant movement of the ship and the lack of hot food. My brandy flask was smashed and when I swallowed three aspirins in the ship's stale water it tasted vile, since the sediment at the bottom of the tanks had been shaken up. Valencia, I kept repeating to myself, we should get to Valencia tomorrow.

It was not yet dawn when I woke, and at once, with a rush of relief and pleasure, I could feel the *Tinos* riding more easily. I grabbed my lifebelt and ran on deck. Not only had the rain stopped but the wind had altered course and the black waves were racing alongside the ship, so that she no longer rolled but dipped with a gentler rocking motion. The water had ceased cascading across the oil tanks and instead it came whipping over the bows in a fine spray. At several places the stars shone calmly through the clouds, and in that bluish light there was a certain splendour in the sea now that the menace had gone out of it.

The captain and the mate were still standing on the bridge looking weary and unshaven. 'Bad goddam night,' the mate said. 'Man broke his leg.' He had been down in the foc'sle again setting the broken shinbone and trying to drug the patient to sleep.

The dawn came up slowly, coating the world at first with cold insipid grey; then with a sudden blaze of yellow the rim of the sun showed on the horizon and every wave-top to the east seemed to be on fire. This was extinguished just as quickly when a cloud came across the sun and there was a last flurry of rain. By ten o'clock the sea was green again and nothing more than choppy; far to the north the mate declared he could see through his glasses the tip of Cape de la Nao. The Cape was no more than a hundred kilometres from Valencia, and eighty from Iviza, the nearest of the Balearics, the island where the *Deutschland* was bombed. In a quick little panic I remembered the bombers and the submarines; this was the critical part, the place where half a dozen other ships had gone down in the last few months. And now the covering storm had gone. We sailed up to the Cape in warm sunlight.

It was impossible now to avoid looking into the sky. One caught oneself at it in the midst of a sentence, even in the act of lighting a cigarette. The bombers, they said, came out of the sun, and I forced myself from time to time to look into its glare, a useless business since one was blinded for a minute or two afterwards.

Slowly we came past Gandia, Tabernes de Valldigna and Gullera, little clusters of white buildings near the shore with the bare brown hills behind. Except for the engineers and the men lying wounded in the foc'sle, most of the sailors were on deck making repairs to the lifeboats after the storm.

But still nothing showed in the sky and we saw no other ship, no sign of danger anywhere. It was utterly unlike the arrival I had imagined; the coast lay placidly sleeping under the warm sun. There were no fires, no wrecks along the beach, no gunboats on patrol, no anti-aircraft bursts in the sky, nor any evidence of war; merely this peaceful sea and the *Tinos* cutting through it as though she were on a holiday cruise. Without so much as a false alarm we came up to Valencia in the late afternoon and began signalling with a Morse lamp to the shore. Two other ships, one British and the other Norwegian, were standing outside the harbour mouth, and their crews were unconcernedly bathing from their sides.

Little by little as we crept through the harbour mouth the grey line of the shore resolved itself into separate buildings, into wharves and docks and little groups of green trees. We could read the Spanish advertisements on

the hoardings and the strong heavy smell of the shore
came across the water. Here and there a warehouse had
been bombed into ruins, and a single siren was still wailing
from somewhere inland. On the streets there were many
people bicycling and walking, and occasionally a car
flashed by in a little cloud of dust. As we tied up two
boats filled with men in bright uniforms came across the
harbour towards the *Tinos* and others ran to secure the
ropes on the dock.

I went down to my cabin and threw my belongings into
my two bags, and then carried them on deck. I had an
overwhelming desire to get off the *Tinos* without a
second's more delay; and I remembered then how the
crew of the *Deutschland* had behaved in Gibraltar.

*

In Valencia no servant would accept a tip. Each morning I
went from my room in the Victoria Hotel to a café in the
Blasco Ibanez and it was the same with everyone who
served me there—the boy who brushed my shoes, the
chasseur who ran for the newspapers, the girl in the telephone box and the waiter who brought the coffee; none of
them would take so much as a centime. And if the money
was left on the table they would pursue you down the
street and hand it back. This was something created by the
civil war, or rather by the belief on the Republican side
that all men are equal. The effect of this was to create a
sensation of freedom and good humour.

Later on I discovered that nearly all people and all
cities undergo a spiritual metamorphosis in a war, that
money loses its value and human beings themselves
become the currency; but here in Valencia where the civil
war had been waged for fourteen months everything to
me was new and surprising. The money itself, like a rich
man suddenly beggared, was no more a matter of solid
coins and impressive banknotes; people were using grubby

little squares of paper which had been recently printed in a haphazard sort of way by the local government. There were also in circulation postage stamps stuck on cardboard, and in some places money had disappeared altogether in favour of barter.

The Spaniards seemed to me to be wildly and irrationally generous; they would welcome any stranger to a meal, they would hand over their last cigarette to a passer-by in the street. Wherever you went you were accepted on trust, and immediately. People had no reticence about their private lives; since everybody was caught up in the same dire emergency and life might end abruptly at any moment the citizens were extraordinarily kind and considerate with one another. There was really nothing to hoard, and no insurance could be taken out against the future. Most of the normal affectations of life had disappeared, so that it did not matter whether you wore a good suit or a tattered pair of trousers, or where you ate your dinner. You shared life intensely with your neighbours; you ran to them in trouble and got their help and called them in to take part in all your celebrations and days of good fortune. Even the spoken word was altered, and from morning to night you talked nothing but politics and warfare.

It was one of those brief moments of ardent communism which overtake all cities in the early days of a war. The old structure of society had vanished, and there had not yet been time for a new hierarchy to take its place. The community was still sharply propelled and even exhilarated by the new danger of life; it had not yet suffered too badly and there was still great hope in the future, a sense that everyone was taking part in a tremendous experiment. There was an element of freewill instead of mass patriotism, and many of my generation felt more deeply about that struggle than we ever came to feel about the world war. It was not so much a feeling of hatred or anger but of deep indignation. We felt that what was happening was evil and unfair and that the fascists must be defeated if there was any justice left in the world. When La Passionaria uttered her cry 'No pasaran' we responded to it absolutely; no, they were not going to pass. We were wrong, of course, but we could not know it as yet.

And so the people in Valencia went about with a feeling of spontaneity and freedom, a feeling of being alive, of discovering one another and life itself for the first time. Later on the monotony would come in, the food would grow shorter, the death and the danger multiply, and the hope would fade; a new military and political hierarchy, harsh, desperate and drastic, would grow up, and all this freshness would fall away. It is not true that people show the best of themselves in the midst of a calamity any more than they do at the height of prosperity; the best comes somewhere in the centre, when the past is put away and they embark on a new experiment and they are willing to suffer any sort of hardship because they believe in what they are doing. This is the enthusiasm of the young farmer sowing his first crop, of a woman bearing her first child, of a community launching itself into war.

Everyone in Valencia, so far as I could see at this time, believed in the war. The city was covered with brilliant and dramatic posters urging the people on to fight. The talk in the crowded cafés was explosive. Cars and buses went careering through the dusty street as though they were bound on the most vital missions of life and death. People snatched at the newspapers as they came out and read them with a fierce and hungry interest. Soldiers were everywhere, both men and women, and they walked about with a certain insouciance and buoyancy which was childish but infectious. They shouted over their single-course meals in the restaurants, they gave the clenched fist salute with the undergraduate earnestness of football players, they wore badges and revolvers, they laughed and joked uproariously or listened with breathless suspense to any new story from the front. In all the squares loudspeakers were blaring out announcements, music was playing, and excited crowds were milling about with that strange throbbing intensity you only see in times of war. Fresh from the staid and cautious world of Gibraltar and the rigours of the *Tinos* I gazed at this animated scene with delight. I savoured the excellent solidity of the ground and even the wailing air-raid sirens had their charm.

Had I now or later ever been allowed to remain in Spain it might have been another story; then no doubt the underlying grimness would have supervened. But this was never permitted to me. My paper already had its staff correspondents at the front, and I, as a very minor employee, never managed to put in more than two or three days in Spain before the foreign editor ordered me back to the safe dull confines of either Gibraltar or France. I was used mainly as a courier to get messages and supplies to the other more important members of the staff, and just occasionally was given some special job which they were too busy or too remote to undertake. I never even got to Madrid. Thus Spain became for me a place of forbidden exhilaration, and I never went down there on one of my flying visits without thinking, 'Please God let something happen to make it possible for me to stay.'

Paris

Quarante-sept bis, Rue Coutureau, St Cloud, Paris, that was the address of the first home of my own I ever had. I moved in one afternoon in May 1938. It was a curiously un-Parisian place to live in; there was no narrow street full of whimsical shops and pungent characters, no music, no street-cries, no bookstalls, no romantic poverty, no smells, none of the famous back-alley decor of the Left Bank. It was more like Sweden: everything brand-new down to the floor boards and the coffee grinder. It was a great battleship of a building on a wooded hill above the Seine, one of those new apartment houses that looked like a sanatorium, and I was the first tenant to move in. My studio on the seventh floor was one of the show pieces of the place; one vast window let the light into the studio itself, my double-room was to the left, and there was a little kitchen just inside the door. Then the stairs went up to a sort of minstrel's gallery or balcony which was perched at the back end of the studio opposite the window, rather like an Elizabethan stage setting. It gave on to my highly polished, chromium-plated rubber-floored bath-room.

Below me—all Paris. I looked down as from an aero-plane so that the city appeared as a plan, or rather a relief map, highly coloured. Directly below, some six or seven hundred feet down, the Seine made a wide sweep round the Renault factories at Billancourt, and all the foreground was filled with the green woods of the river, the race-course at Longchamps, and the Bois de Boulogne. Paris itself floated in a grey mist at the further side of the green belt, and from this height it showed merely as a jagged line of

4*

buildings on the horizon. Here and there the great land-
marks of the city jutted up into the sky, and they looked
like toy models of themselves—the Invalides and the Tour
Eiffel on the left bank, the square block of Notre Dame in
the centre of the river, the Arc de Triomphe on the right
bank, and then, far to the north, higher and more beautiful
than all the rest at this distance, the tiny gleaming
Byzantine domes of the Sacré Coeur on the topmost crest
of Montmartre.

At dusk this all became blurred with a rose and purplish
light like the paintings of the early impressionists, and at
night, especially about midnight, all the valley of the
Seine where Paris lies became a black bowl strewn with
glittering beads of light as though a part of a tropical sky
had fallen on the earth.

Behind me on the hill was the Faisanderie and the Parc
de St Cloud, so that by day in my apartment you had the
effect of perching on the higher branches of the trees, and
by night you seemed to float on yellow light. When
visitors arrived they simply gasped and remained staring
fixedly at the view, which was no bad thing since it took
their eyes off the poverty of my furniture. The beds and
bedding and the pots and pans I bought *en bloc* at the
Printemps, the rugs and curtains (slightly shop-soiled) at
the Galeries Lafayette, the tables and chairs and gadgets
like reading lamps at the Marché aux Puces; and still the
place looked like a struggling doctor's waiting room.

When the cook-valet and houseboy arrived he cast an
atmosphere of extreme sophistication over the apartment.
He was an Annamite from French Indo-China, a slim and
ageless little Buddha, and his tiny features barely broke
the smooth surface of his round hollow head. He spoke
French, wore a starched white coat, and his name as far as
I could gather, was Nam. He demanded 1,500 francs a
month and his keep, which seemed reasonable, since the
rate of the franc then was *150* to the £1; and so I engaged

him. The results were remarkable. When I emerged from
my bath the first morning I found Nam had laid out a
careful selection of clothes for me to wear. As I came to
get into my trousers he held them poised in mid-air for
me to step into. I supposed this was the sort of delicate
attention for which I was paying the 1,500 francs. The
dinner that night, however, was superb. His speciality was
a meal of exclusively Annamite dishes which had to be
consumed by a minimum of six people; it consisted of five
dishes, and was so designed that each dish should overtake the last, so that you ended the meal by eating all five
dishes together.

I found myself slipping into a fairly exotic routine each
day. Nam brought me my coffee in bed and I skimmed
through some twenty of the hundred and fifty Paris
papers—the Blum editorial in the *Populaire*, Kerillis in the
Figaro, Tabouis in *l'Oeuvre*, the *Petit Parisien*, *l' Humanité*,
Le Matin, *Le Journal* and so on. Then down to the garage
beneath the building where the concierge rather cere-
moniously waved me into the Matford. Then to the
Racing Club in the Bois, where I took off my clothes and
lay beside the swimming pool for an hour reading the
remainder of the papers. I enjoyed the rest of the drive
into Paris, and so contrived it that I came in along the
lake and out of the Bois at the Porte Dauphine. From
there you look up the Avenue Foch and see the Arc de
Triomphe three-corner-ways on, and when it is framed in
those glades of trees on a sunny morning I claim that it is
the most beautiful and moving monument in Europe.

Driving in Paris is simple, the technique of the use of
the horn and the brakes and bluff, and when one has
mastered this it becomes easy. The Parisians are not
necessarily dangerous drivers; they drive on flair, taking a
continuous series of nervous last minute decisions and they
are extremely clever. The acceleration of the Matford was
just a little more than that of the Renault and Citroen

taxis, my enemies, and this maddened the drivers beyond endurance. We lined up at the traffic signals at the top of the Champs Elysées, about eight cars abreast, mostly taxis. Then when the gendarme dropped his hand, we leapt forward, jostling for position in the centre of the road like racehorses getting away from the barrier. It was just as well to start immediately cursing the other drivers on the principle that if they had not already done you down they would very shortly do so. And so, amid an uproar of shouts of 'assassin' and 'cochon' and the horns at full blast, we went careering down the cataract of the Champs Elysées from gendarme to gendarme until we reached the wider quieter waters of the Place de la Concorde and the Rue de Rivoli. I arrived much refreshed at the *Daily Express* office around midday.

At one we went up to the bar on the roof for a four-franc *coupe de champagne*, then round to Pierre's for luncheon. At fifty francs a head this was an extravagance, but it was hard to keep away from the most civilized food in the world when it was so near. The chef had lately been achieving triumphs with his kidneys sautés, his wild strawberries soaked in white wine, his coq au vin and his chateaubriand, which was cooked as it ought to be between two pieces of inferior meat over an open fire. Your chateaubriand was actually stewed in its own juice and the juice of the two outer pieces of meat, which were thrown away at the end of the operation. I upset the waiters by insisting on eating my baby potatoes and asparagus tips at the same time as the meat instead of afterwards. As far as possible we tried to limit ourselves to a half carafe of white wine each and one small brandy afterwards.

We never touched whisky or gin; a single glass of beer and perhaps a couple of glasses of champagne was the ration in the office before dinner, and then at eight thirty or nine we dined. Our greatest discovery was the Lapin

Blanc in a little road off the Rue du Louvre. It was a *bistro* rather than a restaurant, and an obese white rabbit did actually prowl about the sawdust on the floor. There was a catch, however; when the chef was sober the food was filthy. Drunk, he cooked like an angel.

Then back to work until midnight. I loved this time; the quiet in the streets below, the silence and the sour smell of wet newspaper ink in our little office, the feeling of intense remoteness in the centre of a restless and crowded city. Usually before I went home I popped into the Café des Sports across the road for a beer with the taxi drivers. The Café des Sports was run by an ex-footballer, and he achieved the most appalling interior decoration in all Paris against fierce competition; it was an L-shaped bar lit by the most harshly brilliant strip-lighting. The banquettes were scarlet leather, and the walls were decorated with scenes from the sporting world. Most of the clientèle leant over the pin-tables and shouted politics at one another with astonishing energy. Half an hour of that and then home in the car.

There was a brief moment when one caught sight of one of the really beautiful vistas of the city. This was in the Place de la Concorde, when you looked up the river of traffic in the Champs Elysées and saw the summer sky through the great arc itself and the dark trees with the headlights weaving in and out, and the crowds in the pavement cafés, and the brilliant dresses of the girls at the cinema entrances, and in the midst of this, Clemenceau—*Le Tigre* himself in bronze with a bronze cape, standing furiously alone but giving the impression of forging into the melée of the Rond Point like the figurehead of a ship.

One or two nights a week I had to go out with business visitors from England. They came into the office with black hats and tightly rolled umbrellas and they had an air of taut and pallid restraint. For a while we talked earnestly about politics and business. Then—'Care for a drink?' Up to the bar on the roof for champagne, with Montmartre in the distance and all the lights of the city below. Your visitor gripped his umbrella and with hunger—that kind of hunger you get from living in the dismal dreary boring cities of England—discoursed on the beauty of Paris and how fortunate were we who lived here. Then—'Don't know whether you're free tonight—got to be in bed early myself—but if you'd care to have dinner—you fellows know all the places—then off to bed—not proposing a wild night or anything like that.'

From this point on it was a prescribed and definite routine. We dine at the Tour d'Argent or Maxim's or the Cigogne d'Alsace and talk firmly about Hitler and the possibility of war. Your visitor opposes a steady British calm to what he clearly believes to be the shifty and un-reliable nervousness of France. No, there'll be no war, he says. It's all a question of oil supplies. It'll be many years yet before Hitler gets his ersatz factories going. Then rubber. We take rubber through a second glass of brandy, and then—'Don't quite feel like turning in yet—don't let me drag you out if you're busy but we might look in for a minute at one of the earlier shows—don't want to be late.'

It was easy enough to get a front table at the Bal Tabarin, especially if you had been there and seen the show ten times before. Here the visitor will not surrender his hat and umbrella to the attendant, but he plants them under his chair where they will be safer. And as though some additional resistance is required to fend off the decadent night-club atmosphere, we return even more resolutely than before to business and politics. What were we discussing? Rubber. Now do I know what tonnage of rubber is required to keep a single division in the field?

Naked, six-foot girls come whirling from the roof and debouching from the walls. They rise in glittering tableaux on lifts beneath our feet and their breasts are not a yard away from the visitor's nose. Girls on horses, girls

in cages, girls in mountains of flowers, girls being flung in
the air by fierce Spanish dancers, girls wearing nothing
but a cache-sexe and a mammoth hat. The band roars and
a young man in silver tights recites a prose poem through
a microphone. We talk rubber. We talk shipping ton-
nages, splits in the Nazi Party, the Italian shortage of
coal, and the new Presidential election in America. We
cast an amused and only faintly interested eye on all these
breasts and thighs and horses, because we are sophisticated
serious people, because the guest is on a business visit to
Paris, that and nothing more, and because England is the
world's last refuge of pornography. Such scenes as these,
in our opinion, can be witnessed only by men, only when
drunk, and only at extremely rare intervals when we are
young. We are not so young as all that and we are certainly not drunk. So we order another bottle of champagne.
And while we wait we turn our chairs a little further
round so that we get a better view of the show.

Out into the Paris night at one o'clock. Taxis and touts
and brilliant lights across the street. Perhaps if we went
somewhere for one quick drink before we go home. Up
the right hand side of the Rue Pigalle; the Jockey night-
club, then the Viking. Down the left hand side; the
Splendide and the Can-Can. The visitor at first will not be
parted from his hat and umbrella at all. He will not even
put them under his chair. He holds them firmly in his hand
and he is annoyed and embarrassed when Fifi, the dance
hostess, tries to put her arm around his neck. But he
relaxes. At the Viking the umbrella goes under his seat
and we talk of the incidence of vice in Paris. At the
Splendide he dances with Fifi and we talk to her about sex.
At the Can-Can Fifi is on his lap, the black hat is perched
on the back of her head, and we don't talk about anything
at all. It is very near the end. It is the moment for me to
rise and say: 'I think I'll be getting along.'

'Oh, don't go yet.' He does not care whether you go or

stay. There are only two things left in his mind; one is a last desperate concession to respectability and the other is the devil himself. The respectability comes first. 'I'll see you in the office, then, at nine,' he says.

'Shouldn't we make it ten?'

'No, old man, it better be nine—got to take the afternoon train.'

Then the devil: 'I say—I'm not often in Paris— suppose I better make a night of it for once—you don't happen to know——'

'Yes. Here is an address. Here it is, I'll write it down on the back of this cigarette packet. Don't go anywhere with Fifi here. Much better to go to this place.'

'Thanks a lot. Good night. Good night. So long old man. See you at nine.'

Home. Home, where the mind was four hours ago. Home, wearily, feeling like a tout. Fur on the tongue, money gone, nothing but an overwhelming sense of aimlessness and lonely despair.

I make the office by ten the following morning, and there he is. He has been waiting a full half hour, sitting upright in the chair, taut, rigid and pale, with his hat and umbrella in his hand, ready to talk business. We do not mention the night before.

I spent one whole day in the woods at Fontainebleau with the murderer Eugène Weidmann. Only the French could have devised such a cat-and-mouse game as this business of getting the criminal to confess before his trial, and only the Parisians could have staged such a grisly *fête champêtre* as we saw that day. The early summer sunshine made long shafts of yellow light between the trees, and the air in Fontainebleau was sparkling. We drove out from Paris in half a dozen cars—the police with Weidmann, the *juge d'instruction*, the clerks and the lawyers and the newspapermen. Weidmann was in the leading car, and suddenly he held up his hand to indicate that this was the spot to which he had brought the sixth and last of his victims. Just why he should have confessed this, why he should help his enemy the French law in this way, is something which I shall probably never understand. Perhaps the desire for confession plus the instinct towards exhibitionism is stronger than we think.

At all events we tumbled out of the cars in the sunshine and when we were assembled on the grass Weidmann explained how he had advertised for a governess in one of the Paris newspapers. Jeanette Keller, a girl who was partly American, had replied and been accepted. He met her at the Gare de l'Est and drove her to this point in the woods. Then he stopped the car and asked her if she would care to see the caves. They had climbed up the hill towards the caves together.

Weidmann explained all this while we stood round him in a ring beneath the trees, and I could not take my eyes away from his eyes. They had that large, moist fidelity of a dog, but with a startling intelligence; and he was so seriously trying to make us understand clearly. Mad? Or simply living in another plane of existence? With a shy movement of his hands (they had taken off his handcuffs) he indicated the track he had taken through the woods and suggested that we should follow. Making little, bird-like gestures, the Frenchmen agreed and we all set off together tramping up the hill behind the murderer. The scene at that moment was a delirious perversion of the hue and cry; here was the quarry brought to bay and still he was the leader. And all these little men who had never broken the law, who would presently be bustling home on the Metro to sit with their faded wives in the suburbs, reading their evening newspapers in their stockinged feet —all these so righteous little men puffed after him up the hill, nodding and chuckling to one another because this was an odd moment in the routine of their lives, because they were peeping deliciously and safely into the terrible gulf of murder. It was like being at the cinema—better, because this was real; here was the murderer, Weidmann, not ten paces off, and still he couldn't hurt you. And presently his head was going to be chopped off. We went up and up through glades of mossy rocks and last year's leaves were still lying on the ground in their autumn colours.

When we reached the mouth of the caves there was a dilemma. No one had thought to bring out electric torches from Paris. The lawyers in their shiny black suits gathered round in a ring to debate this matter, and their sad Daumier faces were as long and foxy as though they were unravelling a point of law in the Palais de Justice. It was Weidmann who solved the problem. 'Has no one any matches?' he said in his soft German accent. 'I think matches would do.'

Down the slimy steps we went; two of the *flics* in front striking matches, then Weidmann, then the judge, and then the rest of us, baying like hounds with excitement and amusement. We arrived in a square rock chamber about twenty feet below the ground. It was a favourite spot for the trippers from Paris, and many of them had scrawled their initials through the damp moss on the walls. The matches flared and fizzled, and the officials tried desperately to keep the proceedings official.

'What then?' snapped the *juge d'instruction*. He was a terrier-like little Frenchman with spiky moustaches and I don't think he liked it very much in the dark.

'I asked her to lean over and inspect the drawings on the rocks a little closer,' Weidmann said. 'Then, while she was leaning over I took my revolver out of my pocket, like this.' He drew his hand up from the darkness with one white finger sticking out to represent the revolver. 'I could show you how.' His voice trailed off vaguely.

'Is there someone to enact the part of Jeanette Keller?' demanded the judge. 'Have the police provided anyone?'

Nobody volunteered so they pounced on a lawyer's clerk who looked the most innocent and feminine in that rugged company.

'Bend over here,' said Weidmann. 'Lean forward and look at the wall.' I could see his great dog-eyes gleaming faithfully in the match-light and his face was in a transport—quite placid and serene but utterly engrossed. Even for us, the ragtail and the bobtail of the Paris system of law, it was not difficult to imagine that we were alone here in the cave with Weidmann and the American girl, Jeanette Keller. We stood quite still and unconsciously suppressed our breathing like an audience watching the crisis of a play, and for the moment there was no other world but this: one felt quite certain that a murder was about to be committed before our eyes and that one was powerless to do anything but wait for the horrible and inevitable end. The lawyer's clerk was sweating; we had one glimpse of his rubicund and comical little face, flinching and twisted with nervousness, before he turned towards the wall. As he leaned over Weidmann lifted up that long white finger and pressed it into the back of his neck. The clerk gave a short cry and tried to straighten himself but the finger pushed him down again.

'And then?' said the *juge d'instruction*.

'And then,' Weidmann said softly, 'I shot her.'

Just for a second I could see the eyes of the watchers peeping like animal's eyes everywhere out of the darkness, the gendarmes with their sweaty hands, the lawyers in their terrible French suits, the ferret-like journalists with their cameras and bundles of newspapers under their arms, and just for that second they had forgotten where they were or who they were; the gendarmes had forgotten that they were gaolers, the lawyers had forgotten to relate this to the law, and the journalists took no account of the fact that this was front-page news. Just for this instant this scene was pure murder with none of the values of society placed upon it; and it was terrifying. Then the matches fizzled out.

'Strike a light,' said the *juge d'instruction*, 'strike a light at once.'

When the first match flared out we could see the lawyer's clerk had risen and was making towards the opening of the cave. With one accord everyone turned and followed him.

A soft-drink seller, attracted by the crowd, had set up his stall in the piercing sunlight outside, and we gathered round him eagerly, lighting cigarettes, buying his sticky, yellow-green syrup. The gendarmes made no attempt to place the handcuffs on Weidmann's wrists again, but they bought him a drink instead. And while he drank he explained what he had done with the body. Had he taken her money? the judge asked. Yes, but he had not spent it. Had he had sexual intercourse with the girl before or after the murder? no, he had not done that. Then why had he bothered? Why had he killed her? He began haltingly, but then he stopped and turned away. It was the only question he could not answer. And as he sat there he looked like a poet; he had all the composure of the confessional, all that gentleness and sensibility of someone who is entirely at peace and no longer requires anything of anybody. It was his questioners who looked so strained and anxious. They kept yapping round him, impatiently waiting to jostle their neighbours out of the conversation, glancing agitatedly at their watches, contradicting one another, taking notes and thrusting forward nervously again in fear that they had missed something of importance. They withdrew into little groups and paced about solemnly in the woods. They placed tape measures on the ground. They took photographs. And the *juge d'instruction* looked cross and very worried. He snapped his fingers for the dossier to be brought. He stood and waved his arms. He bustled back to the entrance of the cave again. Weidmann

sat on the wood bench with his unfinished glass of syrup
before him and listened with care to every question.
Finally they put the handcuffs back on his wrists and we
went down the hill together to the cars.

A fortnight later I was at St Jean de Luz (and this was
when I met Alex for the first time). My newspaper sent
me down there on a trip because things looked so serious
in Spain. I couldn't help thinking it would be heart-
breaking if, after two years' struggle, the Republicans
were to collapse at last. Yet it might happen; they were
already broken in the west. Franco's agent in St Jean de
Luz smiled and smiled, but still he would not give me a
visa to go into Fascist Spain; and so I had to stay there on
the border and learn what I could.

Nearly all popular journalism is an artificial trick of
presenting facts at second-hand, but this was fourth or
fifth hand work. I listened in my bedroom to the Spanish
radio stations, I read the Spanish papers when they came
across the border from San Sebastian, I talked to the
refugees and travellers passing in and out; and I lunched
and dined with the diplomats. But I saw nothing. I underwent no emotional or spiritual experience. I did not
expose myself to the war I was writing about. The war,
for me, was a crackle on the radio, a jumble of headlines in
a newspaper, an improbable twice-told tale from an unresponsive refugee; a dim diplomatic theory muttered
across the aperitifs on a sunny morning by the beach. I was
not really writing about the war at all; I was writing about
the war as it was reflected there in safe St Jean de Luz, and
I might just as well have been looking at the reflections in
London or New York or Moscow.

There are only two aspects of a war (or any other event)
worth writing about; the war as it actually is before your
eyes, and the actions and mental behaviour of the men con-
trolling it. There on the Spanish border I saw neither the
men who were fighting nor the politicians who directed

them. The news filtered through to me in a fog of propaganda, and it was not even clever or predictable propaganda. Some days a few gobbets of truth or imagined
truth lay carelessly on the top of it. At other times the
facts were buried erratically at the bottom. But each night
I went off and pinned down what I could into a few careful
little clichés and sent them off to London. Each night I
said to myself: perhaps tomorrow will yield something
true. Finally I decided to drive off into the central
Pyrenees on a vague hunch that something was happening
there.

There is a quality of gladness—the 'riant' of the Guide
Bleu and the Baedeker—about the Pays Basque and the
Basses Pyrenees in the early summer that makes you
wonder why you waste your time living in any other place.
When I drove up to Bayonne that day and thence eastward along route 117 to Pau and Tarbes I saw nothing,
for mile after mile, but the vineyards framed in the white
trunks of the plane trees; and beyond this, to the south,
the Pyrenees. Every village was swarming carelessly with
farmyard animals, every peasant's cart was piled with
bright vegetables and fruit. It is this abundance in the sunshine—the sense that there is always enough and something to spare—that makes the gladness. It is not the
teeming and extravagant anarchy of the tropics, and it is
not the wretched caution of the north, where every sheep
has a name and every duck is carefully herded into its pen
at night, but something in between, a luxuriance con-
trolled.

Since I drove parallel with the Pyrenees all day I found
myself constantly shifting my eyes from the minutiae of
the villages to that fabulous horizon of shining white
peaks in the distance, a sort of heaven-and-earth experience. In the villages everything is brought up into fine
detail, the yellow dog lying asleep in the roadway, the
peasant women plonking their baskets of washing on the

river stone, the duck with wings outstretched standing
like a ballet dancer on the water, the farmer's boy pissing
against the red brick wall. Each petty thing is significant,
temporary, imperfect and intimate. Then you lift your
eyes to the mountains. Here and there is a low cloud
caught by a sudden uprush of air, and it streams off the
crests with the effect of a horse's mane flying in the wind.
You may notice one or two other details like that; but
really it is the sheer immensity of the Pyrenees which fills
the mind, the superhuman purity, the perfection and the
timelessness.

It was already three o'clock when I got to Montrejeau
in the Hautes Pyrenees and then turned directly south into
the foothills. Within an hour I had climbed into the pine
forests, the summer dropped below, and I felt a dank chill
on my skin. There were odd chunks of snow lying between
the trees, and presently as I went higher these grew together until the ground was one continuous sheet of white
with snowdrifts deepening on the road. I put on my
sweater, then gloves and coat and scarf, and still it was
cold. By the time I got into Luchon my teeth were
chattering.

Luchon, normally, was a crowded, cheerful place, I
imagined, full of holiday-makers. But June was too late for
ski-ing, too early for the summer season. And so the
hotels and pensions stuck up out of the snow, gaunt,
shuttered and empty. Many of the villagers had closed
their shops and surprisingly were plodding upward towards the last pinnacles of the mountains above the town.
There were an unusual number of police about, and when I
stopped and asked what was happening, they waved me on
vaguely: '*Les Espagnols, les refugiés. Vous verrez.*'

Beyond Luchon even the pine forests fall away, and you
come at last to a fantastic semi-circle of snow and ice
which marks the topmost crest of the central Pyrenees and
the border between France and Spain. Usually this is a

place of silence and utter desolation, but that day at five o'clock there was a continuous stream of people making their way upward. I left the car in the snow and walked on with them to the top, where we looked down into Spain itself, a vast and frightening chasm broken by many sheer precipices of solid ice and white ravines that fell down out of sight.

Peering down into that chasm we saw the Spanish refugees. There may have been a thousand of them, perhaps five thousand, or even more. They were toiling slowly up towards us, and seen from this height they made a long line against the snow. It was a line that kept breaking and rejoining itself, growing fatter and thinner, wavering, stopping and then coming on again. At the steeper places the leaders hacked steps into the ice, but some stumbled and rolled backward out of sight. Others, apparently too exhausted to go on, turned aside into the snow and lay there—so many stationary black dots beside the moving line.

We who stood on the summit—about a hundred and fifty Frenchmen from Luchon, the gendarmes and one or two stray visitors like myself—all of us feeling warm and safe, stood without speaking in the snow and watched. There was an officer from the *Gardes Mobiles* in his black leggings and a red stripe down the side of his breeches, standing at the edge of the crowd, much exercised by his duties. He wiped his hand across his moustache. 'They come to seek the hospitality of France,' he said pompously. 'It is the remnant of the red divisions. They have been cut off by the Spanish National forces.'

When the first of the Spanish finally reached us on the summit we saw with surprise that nearly a third of them were not soldiers but women and children and elderly people, and they carried with them the most intimate and absurdly impractical goods, such as a canary in a cage, a flat-iron, a coloured vase, an embroidered shawl, a dog suffering with frostbite, a parcel of books—anything, in fact, that a refugee might have snatched up at the last moment, not because it was of any practical use, but because he loved and valued it. They clung to these things, feeling no doubt that they represented something saved in the general loss, something that made a bridge between the happy past and this present misery, something that placed them as individuals in the surrounding confusion. Many of these people were wounded or suffering from exposure since they wore the thin clothes of the valleys below, and there were little groups knotted together where a man was being half carried by his friends, or a woman and child were being assisted with tugs and pushes across the snow. Perhaps more than anything else one was affected by the extraordinary kindness and solicitude they showed to one another when they were so weak.

They came up quite silently to the French border, expressing no surprise at finding us waiting for them there, offering no explanation, revealing neither relief nor joy nor excitement. They simply stood like animals in the snow and waited. And we on our side, the group of Frenchmen standing about in a semi-circle, watched them curiously, without at first making any sign of welcome or pity.

The *Gardes Mobiles* were exceedingly efficient. They went up to the Spaniards and took away from them their rifles and pistols and leather pouches of ammunition. The Spaniards made no resistance, and as more and more of them arrived the piles of rifles and bayonets grew steadily higher in the snow, in the form of a pyramid. Next, the refugees were taken to an open log fire, where two big cauldrons of soup were steaming, and this was silently ladled out in tin mugs as each man and woman came by. Then there was a third ceremony which consisted of dusting the refugees with some kind of disinfectant powder.

They stood like dogs while the police peppered them with the stuff. Finally they were formed into squads of perhaps fifty people each, and marched downward to Luchon, one gendarme leading the way in front, another with a sub machine-gun following behind.

All this was done efficiently and neatly in the same unnatural silence. It was as though everything had been rehearsed before, as though everyone knew their place and what was expected of them, and so there was no need for argument or explanation.

When some six or seven of these companies had gone down the mountainside into France I noticed a really distinguished man among the Spaniards. He was very thin and gaunt; he wore the most curious sort of leather knee-boots and a uniform which I took to be that of a major or even a colonel in the Spanish army. He was very tired, much too tired to assert his authority. He stood dejectedly between two peasant women and a soldier, his head bowed down, and dirty blood was seeping through a bandage on his arm. All round him the other refugees who had just arrived were supporting themselves in the same way, some of them crying quietly with the pain of the cold, some merely staring woodenly while they waited for an order to be given. But it was this wounded Spanish officer who especially caught the attention because his humiliation seemed more complete than for the others, and his pride had had so much further to fall. Once, no doubt, he had been a great commander in the field. Now he was being contemptuously pushed about by the French like all the others. A Spanish colonel wasn't worth a row of beans this side of the border.

My friend, the pompous little officer of the *Gardes Mobiles*, formed up this squad with the same precision as the others. He posted one of his men at the front, another at the rear. He opened his mouth to give the order to advance, and then suddenly he too caught sight of the dejected Spanish colonel in the sixth row. He hesitated. Then he did an astonishing thing. I was standing only a yard or two away so I heard and saw what happened. He marched up to the colonel, saluted stiffly, and said in Spanish:

'Sir. Excuse, me sir. Would you care to lead your men down to the valley.'

Afterwards, when the day had gone and the last refugee had descended the mountain and I had thought about the matter again and again, I still did not understand what tug of conscience, what sudden delicacy of feeling could have prompted that sensitive and kindly gesture. It was the only gesture that could have gone home to the heart at that moment, and it was so utterly unexpected that no one there understood it at first, least of all the Spanish colonel.

'What?' he said vaguely. 'I don't understand.'

The *Garde Mobile* waved his hand to the head of the column. 'Would you care, sir, to lead your men to Luchon?'

This time not only the colonel understood, but all those in the ranks as well. He saluted, and as he came past me to take his place in front he had his head up, and it seemed to me that he had forgotten about his wounded arm, his exhaustion, and even perhaps his defeat. And when he gave his orders from the head of the column and the Spaniards recognized the familiar voice, they stooped and quickly grabbed up their bundles from the snow as if they had suddenly woken from a trance. They came to attention with a kind of ragged dignity, waited for the next word of command, and then stepped forward together. The colonel did not look back to see if they were following. He marched ten paces ahead, swinging his one good arm, and it was not possible to watch that pathetic figure in the blue boots or see the pride in the tattered men behind him without breaking into tears.

At all events, we, the onlookers, burst into an emotional

cheer as they went by; and from that instant everything became easier and more friendly. Just for the moment the French had forgotten their *'sales étrangers'* attitude, and they made these poor Spaniards welcome in Luchon. That night they were fed and billeted in various compounds round the town. The next day, I was told, each one was to be given the choice of either returning to Republican Spain by way of Port Bou to take up the struggle again, or of being sent to Franco's newly conquered territories in the east—which meant that they accepted defeat. I for one would not have blamed them in their extremity if they gave up the struggle and submitted to Franco. Perhaps this was the choice before all Europe—and Europe's governments did not seem to be taking very heroic decisions at the moment. It is so easy to give in, so easy to accept; to be indifferent if you are not hurt. It is the loneliness of taking a courageous decision which is the worst part, the necessity for turning yourself against the laissez-faire of the crowd. And in return for being an individual you get nothing but pride.

From the way those Spaniards marched down the hill behind their colonel that afternoon I did not think they would yield. This was the first time I had seen refugees *en masse*, and it filled me with a sense of hopeless inevitability. I felt that this scene was going to repeat itself in one form or another over and over again, like one of those children's games in which you shake the board and the same coloured beads rearrange themselves in another pattern; and so on and so on, with infinite variations. Everything I saw that evening would re-appear; the same characters, the *Gardes Mobiles* and the Spanish colonel, the bewildered crowd, the emotional loyalties, the helplessness, the fear, the pain, the exhaustion and the pride; and here and there the story would be lighted perhaps as it was that day by some simple act of human kindness, perfectly timed and perfectly accepted.

To the Edgware Road   IV

DURING THAT first summer in the desert—the
summer of 1940—Alex and I usually contrived to
get back to Cairo at least once a month. Sometimes
it took us two or three days' hard driving, but always the
crowning moment came up at the journey's end: the sight
of Mena House and the Great Pyramid across the sand.
Then we knew that within the hour we would be sitting in
hot baths and anticipating all the other pleasures that were
to follow, cool drinks, clean clothes, the mail from home, a
long exotic dinner at Shepheards.

Cairo in those days was irresistibly comic. The city was
a vast, sprawling, incoherent anachronism, and it had no
real contact with many of the contemporary events which
for the moment dominated its life. There might be tanks
and armoured cars outside the Kasr-el-Nil barracks, but
flocks of goats and camel teams still passed through the
city by night, and the last camel usually had a red hur-
ricane lamp tied to its tail. Once in the Boulac we saw an
enormous ape sitting complacently on a donkey cart
among a dozen women, all heavily veiled in black. One
could never quite reconcile the extreme modesty of the
respectable women (in the trams they were even herded
into their own special compartment, a sort of travelling
harem) with the abandoned performances that went on,
before entirely male audiences, in the nightclubs every
night.

One girl, named Carioca, was considered a great artist.
She could undulate her stomach tirelessly for upwards of
half an hour, and if you watched her long enough she
created a trance-like effect which transported the mind

beyond all thoughts of sex into a kind of helpless coma. It was caused partly by the whining, throbbing music, partly by the heat and the slowly warming beer we drank, but most of all by the agitated, cat-like rhythm of her brown body. She never moved her shoulders. She came gliding in with a jingle of beads, impassive and upright, and then, when the music quickened, an expression of unbearable agony came over her face. She modestly raised her open hands before her eyes to hide her shame at the awful thing she was about to do, and at that moment her breasts heaved as though they were being inflated and deflated from within and her bare stomach jerked back and forth in an apparently uncontrollable convulsion. The soldiers of the Army of the Nile looked on with glazed eyes and made quite a show of pretending that this was nothing more than an artistic dance and not (as it actually was) a representation of the sexual act in an upright position. After a while the military authorities found it expedient to put the more exuberant of these places out of bounds.

Outside the town the fellahin in their mud-hut villages never changed their ways by one iota; events such as the annual flooding of the Nile and the fast of Ramadan constituted all the world they knew, and they certainly did not care who won or lost the foreign battle in the desert. Among the city dwellers perhaps it was a little different. The war was bringing unbelievable wealth into these ramshackle streets, and the Egyptians, stirred up like ants from their normal torpor, ran hither and thither, gathering in the piastres as they fell. They loved the war and were in a fever to make the most of it while it lasted. There was no black-out, no bombing (Mussolini had a Fifth Column in the town) and food was abundant and cheap. At Groppi's café Levantine women with dark patches under their eyes gobbled sweet cream cakes, and it was as though gluttony, like all the other deadly sins that had been banished from the desert, had redoubled here in this precarious oasis on the Nile. Who knew if ever again one would eat a cream cake once General Rommel advanced to the Delta? What folly to die leaving behind untouched this wealth of possible pleasures. Money, perhaps, you could not take with you into the next world, but at least you were entitled to satiety in this. This was a theme that Alex and I were to take up again much later after the war was over.

Alexandria too had its voluptuous charm. It was generally conceded to be the more sophisticated of the two cities of the Delta; its food was better, less stained with the reek of the kerosene stoves upon which all the cooking was done. Its nightclubs were more cosmopolitan, its society more intelligent, and the sea breeze blew. Yet it seemed to us to lack something of Cairo's spawning, ant-heap intensity, and it had a disturbing nautical outlook upon the lost world of Europe, whereas we in Cairo were concentrated upon the desert and the Nile. In the desert we used to speak with contempt of the cities of the Delta, but secretly I think we loved them. The Sodom and Gomorrah atmosphere, or at any rate our illusion of it, was exactly what we wanted after the austerities of the front; we had a fund of health and innocence to squander. Yet, had we only known it, we were extreme provincials in vice. We did not really want to get drunk and very few of us ever visited a brothel.

Each evening in Cairo, at dusk, Alex and I went to the underground billiards room at the Turf Club. There we ordered just one drink and played billiards for precisely half an hour. The scores were always about the same; Alex made 75 and I myself 44. It never bored us. Each day we approached the inevitable result with excitement, and we enjoyed the sight of the cool green cloth and the noise of the colliding balls. And when this little ballet was complete we went off to dinner. Alex won nearly all the games we played. He was better than me at tennis, much better

at golf (he had played with a handicap of two for Balliol),
and it was only at games of chance that I had the better of
him. He was not very lucky.

As the first summer and autumn went by we began to
experience a sense of remoteness from the contemporary
world. Nearly all Europe by now had fallen to Hitler, the
direct route to England through the Mediterranean was
closed, and the sea journey round the Cape of Good Hope
took many months. We listened to the BBC each evening,
but it was difficult to convert the news that St Paul's
Cathedral and the Strand were being bombed into a clear
visual image. In one way this isolation was of advantage
to Alex and myself; it was almost impossible for a civilian
to obtain an air passage from England to the Middle East,
and consequently our editors were unable to replace us
with more experienced and better known correspondents.
They were obliged to give us our chance, and it was an
important chance, since the desert had now become the
only active front where the British were fighting the
enemy. We knew this and we worked hard; and here
existed the only area of jealousy between us. We were
constantly trying to outdo one another in the dispatches
we sent to our newspapers, and later on, in the books we
wrote. It was a cross-current beneath our friendship, a
kind of private, professional bitterness. We never rejoiced
in one another's successes, we enjoyed hurting one
another. I was always secretly mortified when Alex got a
telegram of congratulation from his editor, and if by
chance it was the other way around he became abstracted
and irritable for a time. This was childish, of course, but it
was there and we cordoned it off from the rest of our lives.
Each day we took up the struggle against each other again,
and we only desisted when we were threatened by competition from outside. Then together we turned our
combined resources against the intruder.

In the autumn a new factor came into our lives. My

wife, who was expecting a child, had succeeded in getting a sea passage from England to South Africa, and she now cabled me that she hoped to fly on to Cairo. I tried to describe Lucy to Alex, and I kept repeating that they were sure to like one another very much. But clearly this was a matter that neither of us could decide upon in advance. Mentally by this time I was more married to Alex than I was to Lucy. As yet perhaps our friendship did not go very deep, but it was based upon a web of recent experiences that could hardly be shared with anybody else, and it was a good deal more than the intimacy which two strangers, coming together spontaneously and fortuitously, can sometimes build up on a long ocean voyage. It seemed now, with the arrival of my wife, that this particular journey might be over, that our friendship could not admit a third person without falling away or breaking up altogether. Neither of us spoke of this, but as the day of Lucy's arrival approached Alex began to retire into a defensive reserve. He arranged to be away for a few days so that she and I could have our first meeting alone. Nothing was decided when he went away; we had not even settled the question of whether or not we should continue to live together.

Lucy arrived by flying-boat at the hottest and most trying moment of the year when the Nile is in flood and the humidity rises. A sandstorm was hanging about, and it made the atmosphere almost unbearable. She came by launch across the brown choppy water of the river to the landing stage, wearing a shapeless blue and white maternity dress. I had seen her last as a slim active woman in London, and now this blue and white bundle was helped by black Egyptian hands on to the wharf.

It was extraordinary that she should have been there at all. The baby was due to be born in a month or two, it was extremely difficult for any woman to get a passage northward from South Africa into the war zone, and she had

had a fearful trip. She needed comfort and rest and re-
assurance that someone would now look after her. I took
her to my hot quarters in the Carlton Hotel. The cold
sliced meat on the luncheon table was beginning to curl up
at the edges, and the buffalo butter had melted into an
amber pool. We could not eat. The flies coursed round in
endless circles under the ceiling. It was Alex who had
reminded me to buy flowers, but these made no show in
that hot air; it was too hot even to sleep.

Lucy had a shower and revived a little towards evening.
I took her then to an open-air restaurant in the city and
told her about Alex. I imagined that I had brought him
casually into the conversation, but it was apparent at once
to us both that here was another effort she must make,
perhaps a major effort, and that somehow for my sake this
stranger would have to be accepted. And yet at that
moment it did not seem possible that she could make any
further effort at all; it was already more than enough that
she had to cope with the wretched room in the hotel, with
the flies, and with the heat.

Alex came back next day and they met listlessly and
perfunctorily. He was busy with a series of articles he was
writing, and we did not see much of him. He arrived
briefly for meals and the three of us talked politely. Then
he disappeared to his room to work or went out with other
friends. From Lucy I could extract only, 'He seems very
nice.' When I drew Alex aside he answered quickly, 'Yes,
I like her very much', and went on to speak of something
else.

At the end of a week I had to go back to the desert. For
some reason this was one of the few trips which Alex and
I had not planned together, and I left him alone with Lucy
one early morning at the hotel. I was away only a few
days but the desert was a wonderful place for clarifying the
mind. It would be disastrous, I saw, to force intimacy upon
two people who clearly did not like each other very much.

Now that I had grown used to Lucy's presence I began to experience a sympathy for her that I had not felt at first. After all, Alex could get along very well by himself. He was the one who had to go.

Once this decision was taken I hurried back to Cairo in a much easier state of mind, and Lucy and Alex met me at the hotel. Both of them seemed brisker and more relaxed than they had been before. I bathed, we went to a restaurant together, and they began to tell me the news of Cairo. They had some private joke about the Levantine porter at the hotel, they had been shopping together in the bazaar and had gone to a party the night before. Lucy now said decisively that we could not continue to live in the hotel; we would have to find a flat which would be cooler and more comfortable. I had been dreading this, for it meant the breaking up of the haphazard communal life with Alex, the establishment of a rigid home with an Egyptian cook and set times for meals, but it was one of the things that I had brought myself to accept while I was away in the desert. I was about to agree rather gloomily when I was astonished to hear her say that she and Alex had already been looking for flats together, and had in fact found a possible place on the bottom floor of an apartment block on Gezira Island. It seemed to be accepted that one of the bedrooms should be reserved for Alex.

We moved in a few days later. It was Alex and Lucy who bought the furniture and engaged Mohammed, the cook, and Achmed, the house-boy. Between them they settled the daily menus, paid the bills, and dealt with the tradesmen. Later on when the baby was born it was Alex, the boy's godfather, who looked after him on the nurse's day off. More often than not it was Alex, not me, who bowled him over the Gezira lawns in his perambulator and who got up to quieten his crying in the night.

Perhaps it was their common pessimism that brought Lucy and Alex together. They both lived as it were in the subjective mood and disliked taking decisions. Mine was the indicative, even the imperative approach, and although I was often wrong (they usually sided against me in an argument), they needed me just as much as I needed them; and so we went on safely together. We seldom if ever visited other people in their houses; we preferred to remain at home, and although we often entertained there we were usually content to be alone together.

But as time went on Alex and I found it increasingly difficult to get back to Cairo for more than a few days at a time, for in December the British Army invaded Libya, 500 miles away. Who can tell you now about the battle of Beda Fomm? Most Englishmen have never heard of it. Yet it was the climax of the first and perhaps the most decisive British victory in the war. At Beda Fomm, just south of Benghazi, the Italian Army was finally routed and a large part of it made prisoner. The Italians never fully recovered from this defeat, and never again after this did the British enjoy such a headlong pursuit or know such immediate and overwhelming success. These were wonderful days. All our fears were swallowed up in the excitement, and as the army overran one enemy camp after another we discovered the immense joys of looting. We looted parmesan cheeses as big as cartwheels, and tins of strawberries, barrels of wine and cases of chocolate, binoculars and typewriters, ceremonial swords and Italian money galore.

We were laden with this loot one day in the hills outside Barce, in Cyrenaica, when we ran into an ambush. There were four of us travelling in a single truck—the driver, Keating, Alex and myself—and we had gone ahead of the main body of the army to join an armoured car patrol on reconnaissance. Everywhere Italian soldiers threw down their arms and surrendered as we drove on along the macadam road to the west, but we kept on, wanting to advance as far as possible by nightfall. We went on so quickly that we surprised a group of Italian sappers laying landmines on a bend of the road, and as they ran away I heard the British commander in the leading armoured car shout to his gunner, 'Give them a burst.' But the gun never fired. Before the man could take aim an enemy battery hidden in the scrub began shooting directly into our little line of vehicles, and tracer bullets came down the road towards us in continuous streams of bright yellow light. The Italian gunners were only a hundred yards away on a little wooded hill, and in a momentary pause in the firing I heard them screaming to one another.

They blew up the leading armoured car very quickly, and at the same moment our driver, a poor quiet boy from the Midlands who never had any business to be in a war, fell sideways in his seat with a terrible wound in his arm. We dragged him from the truck into a shallow ditch, and Keating ran up and down the road among the bullets trying to find a first aid dressing. Alex and I lay with the wounded man and we saw first our own truck and then all the other vehicles destroyed. A soldier went past us dragging the torso of one of his companions, and presently he too was killed. Keating came back with the dressing and lay down with us, but he was hit twice almost at once, and each time the bullets went in his body made a little convulsive jump. He began to pray. My legs at that time were covered with desert sores, and I fumbled about with my bandages, thinking to use them on the wounded man. But it was impossible to move; the Italians could see us and they went on firing. A bullet ripped through the seat of Alex's trousers, raising a little blood, but he said nothing. It was Keating who got us moving at last. We crawled inch by inch, half pushing and half pulling the wounded driver through a prickly thicket of shrubs, and whenever we showed ourselves in the open a stream of fire came down on us again. It was growing dark and the light of the burning cars grew stronger than the sun.

This was my first acquaintance with death, and I think I can remember it very well. I never thought of surrendering. I thought only: this is too cruel, they cannot realize what they are doing to us. If they were here with us they would see it and they would stop. No one, not even a hungry beast, could inflict harm like this. There could be no hatred or anger in the world which would want to hurt us so much. I thought again and again: 'I am not hit yet . . . I am not hit yet.' I did not pray or think of my past life or of my family; I simply wanted to get away. If I had had a gun I doubt that I would have fired it. I did not swear, except softly under my breath, until the driver cried out pitifully that he was in agony and could go no further, and then I shouted, 'Get on you little bastard.' If I helped my companions at all it was done mechanically and without any real volition; with all my senses I longed for the darkness so that I could crawl away and hide.

We must have covered about fifty yards like this when we came to a ditch and the firing slackened. Our driver for the moment could do no more, so we laid him down on the ground. I took a little glass phial of iodine and broke it over his enormous wound. My hands were shaking so much the whole contraption fell into the blood, the broken glass as well as the iodine. When I picked up another phial Alex took it away from me and broke it in the proper way. Then he bound up the boy and got him to his feet again. It was now dusk, and although the firing had ceased we thought the Italians were coming after us on foot and so we hurried through the scrub as fast as the wounded men could go. Half an hour went by, and as my mortal panic subsided I had another fear; suppose our own troops, coming up the road, took us for Italians, suppose they fired before we could speak? We began raising our voices: 'Are you there? Are any British there?' Out of the darkness at last there was an answering cry, and presently we were riding back to a dressing station aboard an Australian bren-gun carrier.

I do not think that I ever recovered from this incident. Often afterwards we were obliged to put ourselves briefly in the way of danger, but I never again did it with any confidence or even with any feeling of dedication. Whenever I went into danger I did it as a duty or because I thought that others were watching me. With Alex I could never tell. Not long before this he had gone off flying over Sicily with the RAF, and when the midships gunner of his plane was wounded he manned the gun himself and by some miracle—he had poor eyesight—he shot down an enemy fighter. This had to be kept quiet at the time because war correspondents were supposed to be non-combatants, and the Germans would have been quite within their rights in shooting him if he had been captured. But the interesting thing was that he experienced no elation from the exploit, or at any rate he never expressed satisfaction of any kind. Later on he went on other bombing raids as well, usually without telling me beforehand, and as the months went by it became clear that he was one of those men who from time to time have to test themselves in some adventure lest they should grow to fear fear too much.

It was during this campaign that we made a detour one day so that we could camp for the night among the marble columns of Cyrene, and later we travelled inland for two days to see the ruins of the temple of Ammon Ra in the Siwa oasis. Back in the Delta we explored the pyramids and bought coloured prints of the Sakkara murals. Then there was that concert given by the Palestine Symphony Orchestra in a depressing little hall in Cairo. Yet it was astonishing how all that side of our lives became suffocated by the War. The Cairo Museum with the Tutankhamen antiquities was closed, but I cannot recall that we ever entered the Mohammed Ali mosque or Sakkara itself, and although I went twice to Khartoum I never paused at Luxor or Abu Simbel. We were in Palestine and we did not visit the Church of the Holy Sepulchre, and at Baalbek, during the Syrian campaign against the French, we stayed only an hour or two. We never went to Petra.

This early part of the war put an odd sort of censorship upon what is generally known as culture. The present dominated our lives, and there was never time to depart from it; the news seemed to be so much more important than history. Antiquities, for the moment, appeared to have no place, and they were put away out of mind like some precious, fragile vase, not to be seen again until after the war. When civilization itself was in jeopardy it was a luxury and an aberration even to read a good book, and the memory of paintings and music was a useless nostalgia in a world where there were no art galleries or orchestras; to indulge in it was to weaken your ability to endure the present.

Alex, who had read so much, gave up serious reading altogether. Often in the hot afternoon in Cairo I would find him not sleeping but lying, stomach downwards, across his bed with an open book on the floor; and if it was not an arabic grammar it was a guidebook or a thriller which by chance he had happened to find lying about the flat.

Nor can I remember that we were drawn any closer to religion by the war. We discussed it endlessly as we lay in our camp beds at night, but we reached, I think, nothing more than a state of suspended judgement. Fatalism, a kind of mental *laissez-faire*, seemed to be the best armour against fear, since at least it came naturally to us, while a half-pretended faith would have been a little cowardly— and one feared cowardice immensely since we were all so prone to it. Alex, who was much more reverent and at the same time more sceptical than I was, could be wonderfully sardonic about such matters. 'Employer's choice', he wrote after the question Religion? in one of those wartime forms we were forever filling out.

'What's this?' the sergeant asked. 'Employer's choice? That's not a religion.'

'It happens to be mine.'

'What's it mean?'

'Just what it says: I let my employer choose for me.'

'Well, you can't have it in the army.'

When Alex got his form back he was marked 'C. of E.', and that, I suppose, was what he really was, at any rate for all outward appearances.

There was one other aspect of our days in the Middle East, and it has only become apparent to me now that so much has changed and so many years have passed: we were rich and powerful. We believed that we belonged to a superior race of men. It was not only that money to a great extent had vanished out of our lives, since we had no use for it in the desert; we were constantly moving among coloured men whose territory for many years past had been governed by the British. The fantastic speed with which the British Empire has disintegrated since the war has made us forget what things were like in 1940. Wherever we went in the Middle East, whether it was Palestine, Jordan or Egypt, however far we penetrated down into Africa through the Sudan to Kenya and beyond, we remained on what we liked to think of as 'British soil'. Like the children of very wealthy parents it seemed quite natural to us that we should occupy the best houses and hotels, that we should have at our command cars, motor launches, servants and the best food. In these circumstances it was difficult not to think of Africans and Egyptians as people belonging to a lower social order. Even if their poverty and their illiteracy did not set them irrevocably below us they were still inferior because we

5*

were fighting the war and they were not. The British were the committed ones, the fighting cocks, the men with the guns. The others were the camp followers.

I don't think we were arrogant, but then whoever recognizes arrogance in themselves? Alex, at least, made an effort to speak to the people in their own language, and although his politics were further to the right than mine (he saw virtue in Franco) he was much kinder and gentler than I was in his dealings with the Egyptians. He gave money to street beggars, I did not; he listened to what the boab and the suffragi had to say. At the front he spent a good deal of time talking to the prisoners-of-war—he was already bilingual in German, and it took him about three weeks to become fairly fluent in Italian—and he seemed to me to be unnecessarily indulgent towards them. It was not exactly a missionary's or a social worker's conscience that impelled him, but rather, I think, a feeling of being at ease with the underdog, a desire to communicate. Was this because he was diffident with his contemporaries, because he considered himself to be something of an underdog, or at any rate some sort of a misfit? I sometimes fancy so.

Looking back into my own feelings I see nothing but a grey indifference. One made the gesture of handing the water-bottle to the wounded prisoner, but in my case it was an act of self-conscious virtue; I really did not care whether he lived or died. I saddled him with the crimes of Hitler and Mussolini. He was the fallen enemy, and, no doubt sub-consciously, I blamed him for the shame of my own fear at the front. The dead too very rapidly passed me by. One had a pang when some friend was killed, but it did not last; he too became swallowed up in the onward rush of the present and was remembered only with a casual and blurred affection such as we feel for some school-boy acquaintance who has been parted from us in childhood.

In a dressing station one day a wounded Australian soldier with an unlighted cigarette in his mouth chatted with me for a while and then said, 'Have you got a match, dig?' I had no matches but I borrowed a lighter in a moment and lit it. The soldier did not draw on his cigarette, however, because in that instant of time he had died. This surely, it appeared to me, was the way: to go out nameless, unprotesting, probably not in pain, the trivial habit of a cigarette making a last bridge with life. Soon after our ambush in Cyrenaica Alex and I chanced to meet one of our friends at the front. He said in astonishment, 'But you have been reported dead.' Looking into his face I thought I saw there just such an expression as I myself might have worn in his place: surprise, a touch of disappointment, and, above all, a suggestion of indifference now that we had rejoined the living herd.

Was I really as hard-boiled as all this? Or can it have been that for the first time in my life I was entirely absorbed in what I was doing and consequently had no time to spare for others? This first year in the desert was an *annus mirabilis* for me. Like a backward sapling that is transplanted into a rich soil I began to sprout with new growth, and I was probably happier than I had ever been before. At a moment when most people's lives were being frustrated and ruined by the war everything conspired to give me confidence: my marriage, my friendship with Alex, the sudden opening of a new career, even the very wartime air of the desert itself and the sense of freedom it conveyed—the feeling of being able to travel out into the distance far beyond the range of money, of bosses and jobs, and of responsibilities.

Through this first year and the year that followed Alex and I were often parted for quite long periods, and it astonishes me now to remember the casualness with which we accepted these separations. Perhaps we even welcomed them. Any separation in the war was quite likely to be final, and yet, like schoolboys going off in different directions for their holidays, we made the most confident plans about when and where we would meet again. When Alex went off on the expedition to Greece I was at the fall of Addis Ababa. We saw nearly all the desert campaigns together, and continued on to Syria, but we were parted for a while during the invasion of Persia when, for the first time, the western allies joined hands with the Red Army and the Red Navy on the Caspian Sea. Once I went off to India and Ceylon to report on the Japanese offensive in Burma, and Alex meanwhile flew away on some strange jaunt to Lake Chad and the Belgian Congo.

Then at the time of the great retreat across the desert in 1942 there came a major separation. Two years of constant movement had made us very tired, and our editors in London agreed that we should have a holiday, Alex in England, I and my family in America. As things turned out this was hardly a holiday at all; Alex was obliged almost at once to return to the desert where the Battle of Alamein was being fought, and I was sent on the invasion of North Africa. Six months went by before the British First Army in Tunisia made contact with the Eighth Army coming up the coast from Tripoli, but I don't think Alex and I ever doubted that we should meet at the point of rendezvous. This happened in May 1943, when the final rout of the enemy had begun. With a little group of companions from the First Army I made my way down to the town of Sousse, on the Tunisian coast, and we had not been there ten minutes before we had the joy of seeing the first patrols of the Eighth Army come into the town. After months in the muddy Tunisian hills we were pale-faced and wearing thick battledress. These others from the Nile, 1,500 miles away, were dressed in shorts and open-necked shirts and they were burned by the sun to a walnut brown. They were covered in dust, and their blackened tea canteens and cooking pots rattled about on the back of their armoured cars. Our equipment was clean and new, theirs was battered and dirty. They were a colonial army, dishevelled and exultant, coming up from an expedition in Africa; we were of Europe, and relatively new to war. The sergeant in the leading Eighth Army car was not a tactful man.

'Who are you?' he called out.

'The First Army.'

He considered it a moment and then said, 'You can go home now.'

I was a little puzzled not to find Alex with this patrol, and went on foot into the town in search of him. There were a number of desert soldiers about, and presently one of them told me that Alex had been seen down on the waterfront making inquiries for me. We met by the sea-wall, and with Keating and half a dozen others went into a dilapidated wine shop. Everyone was talking loudly, since this was a great day in the war, the beginning of the end of the enemy in Africa. Alex and I sat beside one another, listening to the others. Flies swarmed in the shop and the wine was warm and tasted of raisins. We felt shy, and since it was necessary to talk we talked to the others. Soon however we went outside and began to fall into our accustomed ways. Keating found a house where we could spend the night. I helped the drivers unload the trucks, and Alex went off to the bazaar for a dozen eggs. While he was cooking I took a bottle of whisky from my rucksack and poured our usual ration into iron mugs. I had no kit with me, so I took half Alex's and laid out our two beds in a corner of an upstairs room. When the meal was finished we got undressed and then at last we took up the conversation that had been broken off in Cairo half a year before.

After the surrender of Rommel's army and the fall of Tunis we had a day's looting in the Cape Bon Peninsula. The enemy soldiers stood about listlessly in the scrub with all their paraphernalia around them. It was our last looting in Africa. We selected a German volkswagen, piled it high with wines, cameras, tinned food, typewriters, binoculars and clothing (all of which we were subsequently obliged to surrender), and then set off on the three days' drive down the coast to Algiers. We were alone. When it was hot we stopped and dived into the sea. At night we slept in farmhouses and cooked extravagant meals. In the morning in the bright sunshine we went on again. There was no sound of firing anywhere, hardly an aircraft in the sky. We put down the windscreen of the volkswagen so that the wind rushed past our faces.

*

When the army crossed over to Sicily after three years in Africa I was away in England, but Alex landed on the island with the invading troops and I followed him three weeks later. I found him in a correspondents' camp on a dusty plain outside Lentini. He had pitched his bed under one of those formal orange trees which one sees so often in Italian frescoes and medieval woodcuts. It was perfectly symmetrical: a thin straight trunk, a circular cushion of dark green leaves and the ripe fruit hanging from the branches like yellow lanterns on a Christmas tree. The late afternoon sun had long since chased the shade from his bed, but he was fast asleep under his mosquito net.

All this was very theatrical and strange, and Alex himself appeared to be somewhat altered. He was thinner and paler, and clearly he was exhausted by the battles of the past three weeks. When he roused himself and began to tell me about his adventures he disclosed an air of wariness, a certain inward preoccupation. The transition to Europe, he said, had been unexpectedly upsetting. Things here were very different from the desert. And as though to prove his point we were startled, just as dusk fell, by the sound of an Italian voice frantically calling for help. Pre-

sently a contadino arrived, and he was on the edge of
hysterics. He declared that a *goum*, one of the terrible
Berber tribesmen the French had brought with them into
Sicily, had broken into his farmhouse on the hill and was
now locked in an upstairs bedroom with his eldest
daughter. She was screaming. We put the man into a jeep
and drove with him to his home. Gingerly we went up the
stairs and tried the locked door. There was no sound from
inside and we shouted to the *goum* in French to come out.
There was no answer. The contadino and his wife and
family stood round us, weeping and imploring, as we
battered at the door, but it was very solid and to tell the
truth neither Alex nor I much cared to face an armed
tribesman in the darkness there. The *goums* had a reputation for running berserk and for slicing off people's ears.
We drove off then to the French battalion headquarters a
mile or two away and roused a young lieutenant, who said
he would attend to the matter. In the morning the
contadino was back in our camp and he was distraught.
'Mamma mia! Mamma mia!' he cried. 'I didn't mean them
to do that with him. He was only with her a little hour.'

'What happened?'

'The French took that poor soldier out of the bedroom.
They put him up against the wall of my house and shot
him dead.'

'How is your daughter?'

'She is recovered.'

Yes, things were decidedly different in Europe. The
war was no longer a soldiers' tournament in empty space.
We were among civilians again, shells and bombs fell on
statues and suburban shops, on churches and schools,
instead of on the useless sand. Now for the first time we
were observers of the consequences of war. At the same
time we were much more comfortable than we had been
before, better fed, better housed (we soon moved from the
open fields into hotels and billets), and life, though much

more complicated and agitated, became infinitely more amusing. We crossed the Straits of Messina, and as we moved northwards through Italy every lull in the fighting found us established in some relatively comfortable villa with a good cook and a cellar of wine. The winter was bleak and muddy, and the campaign was not very successful, but I don't think that we pined for the dry simplicities of the desert; all that early part of the war was put away from our memories as something too primitive, too provincial, to speak about, and it was only years afterwards that we realized that the desert had far more meaning for us and more influence upon our lives than the final chaotic struggle in Europe.

It surprises me now that my friendship with Alex should have withstood so many new pressures that were put upon it directly we crossed the Mediterranean. We were surrounded by new friends and by endless distractions. Perhaps it was settled habit that kept us together, perhaps it was the continual suffering around us. Everywhere one went the Italians were reaching up their hands and begging: 'Pane. Biscotti. Caramelle.' They swarmed in their ruined houses, emaciated, wretched and dirty, and yet they had a marvellous power of resilience; one cigarette and they were smiling again. Now more than ever we were the privileged class.

Alex had never really liked the desert, and had simply forced himself to put up with it. Now he was returning home to the things he knew. We had roast chicken and chianti instead of bully beef and tea, baroque churches instead of tents and bedouin huts. Once again he was among people whose language he knew so well, and our journey up through Italy was for him a series of recognitions of the past: this was the European returning from exile.

For myself, on the other hand, the desert had been no penance. My Australian background had enabled me to accept it far more easily than Alex. It was a physical life in the open air, uncomplicated by foreign languages and unfamiliar political entanglements, and this, more or less, was the atmosphere in which I had grown up. One's loyalties then were very clear, one's emotions undisturbed. In short, I felt at home with the army in the desert, and consequently I usually had the advantage of Alex there.

But now the boot was on the other foot. Now we were forced to contend with a much more complicated existence, where one lived, conspiratorially, indoors for a great deal of the time, and no issue ever seemed to be entirely clear. I was not quite philistine enough to despise Europe, but the veneer of European-ness I had acquired before the war was thin. I was not entirely at ease there, as Alex was. Consequently from this time forward there was a decided shift in our relationship. He ceased to develop, or at any rate he ceased to explore: instead he was eagerly returning to his own past—not exactly to himself as he was before the war, but to an extension of himself as he was then. I on my side was forced to change and learn and adapt myself more than ever. Perhaps this was made easier for me by the war which ruthlessly opened most doors in all the countries we were about to penetrate, yet it was an exhausting process, and often I was irritable and mentally breathless while Alex continued calmly on his way. In just one aspect I continued to have a firmer footing than he had: the terms of my life were settled. I was married, I now possessed a home in England, and there was never any question about what I was going to do after the war was over. I was going to write. But Alex was alone and undecided. For the moment he was doing very well, in restoring himself to the familiar fields of his past. But might he not end up at that point where I had found him in Athens so long ago: still alone, still a dilettante of many different things and a dedicated professional in none?

This I think created a certain uneasiness in his mind and poisoned a little the pleasant prospect of renaissance palaces, of olive groves and of gracious living, that now lay before us on the mainland of Europe. We did not go into these matters very closely at the time—perhaps they never rose above the level of our consciousness—yet they persisted, and they created a slight strain between us. In all else, however, we were now more than ever together.

We took a truck and drove from the toe of Italy to the Allied bridgehead at Paestum. We lived at Bari for a time, and explored southwards to Otranto and Lecce on the Adriatic. When Naples fell we settled with our friends in a comfortable apartment in Posillipo, and fattened a turkey for Christmas. As yet we had had hardly a glimpse of the long cold nightmare of the war in northern Europe, but we knew it lay in wait for us and it made us cautious. When an eager young officer informed us that we had been chosen to take part in the assault landing of Anzio which was to precipitate the fall of Rome we told him that we did not want to go. We knew that very shortly we should have to return to England for the second front (we did not yet know that it was to be a landing in Normandy), and we had no intention meanwhile of exposing ourselves in a sideshow in Italy.

Looking back on this incident now I ask myself, 'Did we really take ourselves as seriously as this?' And I suppose the simple answer is that we did. The second front hung over us like the prospect of a major surgical operation that one keeps putting off from month to month, even from year to year. And yet we knew we had to face it in the end.

As things turned out, the second front proved to be for us something of an anti-climax. In the spring of 1944 we went up to London to await the day. Alex went down with jaundice at the last moment and missed the landing altogether. I myself meanwhile was plucked by a muscular soldier off a landing barge and was dumped on the Normandy beach without so much as getting my feet wet. That night in London Alex and Lucy, true as ever to their pessimism, conjectured that I might be dead. I was not; I was eating a six-course meal at the Lion d'Or Hotel in Bayeux. Alex arrived a few days later, and so we went on together through the Normandy battles to Paris and Brussels.

The success of the second front had curious effects. Having survived the operation which we had so much dreaded we became more cheerful and yet more selfish, more materialistic than we were before. After four years of campaigning we had lost our resilience, and now more than ever we became cautious; peace at last was coming very near, and it would have been foolish, we thought, to be killed by a stray bullet at the end. We were bound of course to expose ourselves at the front for a few hours every day, but we tended now to let other vehicles run to the head of the column and explore the unknown bend in the road ahead. We lived in comfortable safe billets behind the line, at first in the Lion d'Or at Bayeux and then in the Canterbury Hotel in Brussels, and there in the evening, sometimes for hours at a time, we played a war game called *l'Attaque*. (Did we think perhaps that by moving the cardboard pieces about, by making a game of these make-believe manoeuvres, we kept the real war at bay?) We had sessions of reading poetry and plays aloud, and Alex achieved a very creditable translation of Ronsard's *Quand vous serez bien vieille, au soir, à la chandelle.* For the first time I began to think of money and the things that money could buy, and although we still worked hard we were now more concentrated upon ourselves than upon the war. We tended to be more sickened by ruins than stimulated by danger, and skirmishes at the front which once would have filled our day's horizon now often seemed to us repetitive and useless folly.

Yet I fancy that these days were, for Alex, the best time of his life. He was much more confident. The war had made his reputation as a newspaper correspondent, and he was surrounded now by friends and acquaintances who liked him very much. He was no longer so cautious with money nor did he now find the need to assert himself by barking at minor officials. The slightly suspicious look had gone out of his face, and so many years of living in the open air had given him a certain casual decisiveness in his movements. He was very sunburnt. But the real reason for the change that now overtook him, the metamorphosis that drew him out into the world from the doubts and introspections of his own mind, was the arrival of Robert Graves' daughter Jenny. She came over to Normandy as an officer on the women's side of the RAF, and very soon these two were a great deal together. It was the least predictable of attachments and the most inevitable. Jenny was younger than Alex, and she possessed with an almost bewildering completeness those very qualities which were so much lacking in his own life, a natural vivacity, an unaffected assurance in her own social background, a flair for unusual and optimistic decisions and an astonishing energy in carrying them through: a touch of recklessness, an eagerness for life. Alex rose from the depths like a leaping trout, and all at once his hesitations were resolved. They were married in the Savoy Chapel in London just before the last offensive in Germany. Alex was very proud of Jenny. She stimulated him as he had never been before, and now at last he was warmed by an affection to which he could respond completely. For him this was the perfect ending of the war, the best way back to peace.

The last months of fighting in Germany went by, for us, in a bemused and rather frightening confusion. When ruins are piled on ruins, when the end is inevitable and the battlefield becomes a vast camp of inert and desperate refugees, there is not much excitement in victory, merely a desire for rest. They assembled the remnants of the Seventh Armoured Division—that same division which we had first seen go into action in the desert five years before —and it was ordered to lead the British Army into the defeated streets of Berlin. Alex and I decided not to go. We could not bear to see another ruined city. We no longer possessed the necessary emotions for a victory parade. We got into a car and drove back across the Rhine into France, and I can remember feeling a sense of relief rather than elation. Perhaps we were also a little apprehensive. For five years we had lived with the present, and now, after all this time, we were travelling into the future.

*

For the first few years after the war we four—Alex and Jenny, Lucy and myself—met only sporadically. Lucy and I made an extended trip to Australia and Alex continued as a foreign correspondent; I had letters from him written in a bewildering number of places, New York and Miami, Moscow and Prague, Berlin and Warsaw. It must have been somewhere about 1947, when he and Jenny had established themselves in a house in Paris, that I went over from London to see them. We had an idea that we might travel on together to Italy and there search for some place where we could spend the summer and possibly buy a house. A year or two of coldness and rationing in the north had made us long to see the Mediterranean again.

We drove slowly, stopping at every promising village on the Ligurian coast, and when we arrived at Portofino we realized at once that we had reached the journey's end. It was a cold wet day and no one as yet had pulled down the forbidding stone wall that had been erected across the tiny beach during the war. But Portofino was then a lovely place, perhaps the most beautiful little port that has ever been in the western Mediterranean. There were in those

days no tourist buses, no *boutiques*, no yachts in the harbour
or crowds in the piazza. The hills rose up from the sea in
sparkling terraces of vines and bright rocks with the
contadinos' cottages in between, the Castello was de-
serted, and the village life revolved around the cycle of the
seasons. It was as though there had never been a war,
never any real break with the Middle Ages. We walked
up to the topmost peak of the promontory and found there
the ruins of the Castelletto, which had been a look-out post
in the time of the Saracens and more recently a German
gun emplacement. The view down the Ligurian coast was
stupendous. When Jenny and Alex had rebuilt and
furnished the place, and I and my family had rented a
cottage further down the hill, Portofino became for us a
summer home and, for a few months each year at least, a
symbol of what we thought life ought to be. Our wine
may not have been so good as the Bordeaux we had drunk
so long ago at the Bar Basque in St Jean de Luz, nor our
roast duck so exotic, but we had *prosciutto di Parma* and
scampi fresh from the sea, *pizzas* and melons, and Italy was
a warmer and friendlier country than France. We worked,
we took up the post-war craze for painting in oils, we
swam and went shopping in Rapallo; and in the evenings
we danced on the terrace.

But of course it could not last. Alex and Jenny were
forever being called away by their newspaper jobs, and I
discovered that it is difficult to write books when you are
surrounded by people on holiday. Then too, like all seaside
resorts, Portofino was a little sad after the summer season
was over; one wanted then to go inland to more serious
places. I found a villa in the hills above Florence which
was a more congenial refuge in which to work, while Alex
and Jenny continued erratically around the world, perching for a few months at a time first in Rome and then in
London, but never really settling anywhere.

It was something more than a physical separation. After

the war Alex and I had never quite resumed the long conversation, and at Portofino it had become apparent that
we were embarked now upon two different kinds of life:
mine more or less sedentary, isolated and egocentric, his
diffuse, gregarious, a restless pursuit of contemporary
politics. In other words, we had changed places, and most
unexpectedly he now was the man of action while I
rusticated among the Florentine cypresses. He had now
become an influential political journalist, and his life was
crowded with dinner parties and international conferences.
People were beginning to predict for him an editorship of
one of the national newspapers, a career in politics, many
different things.

In 1950 his book, *Enter Citizens*, came out. It is an
examination of the political prospects of Europe, and it is
based upon the thesis that a new figure had arisen in the
world: the mass-produced man. For a thousand years
before 1800, Alex pointed out, the population of Europe
had stood still at about 180,000,000. In 1950 the total had
risen above 500,000,000. These new mass-produced men,
he contended, were destined to convert Europe into a sort
of ant-colony where all the inhabitants were equal and
identical, where no minorities or individualities were
tolerated, where only material values counted and the
creative genius of the human mind sank to rock bottom.
It is an extremely detached essay. 'I set out,' he wrote,
'with no axe to grind, no cause to champion, no prejudice
to justify.' It is also very gloomy. 'All achievement,' he
wrote, 'is anti-climax. Death sets in the minute the
struggle is over.'

He even had a chapter entitled 'The Death of God'
which opens, 'As you fly from Rome to Athens you can see
on your left hand, imbedded in the blue Ionian just south of
Corfu, a long, thin, dull-looking island. Its name is Paxos,
and from it, at the end of the Greco-Roman classical era,
passing mariners heard a great voice cry, "Pan is dead.

The great God Pan is dead.'' The pagan gods were dead. A god dies when no one believes in him any more. Christianity was taking over the civilized world—a new, rigid religion claiming to be of universal validity, insisting on orthodoxy, rigorously suppressing heresies, permitting no freedom of thought. It held Europe in deep freeze for ten centuries—a thousand dark years which produced scarcely one event or invention or work of art that the ordinarily-educated person can mention. Today, by the same definition, the God of Christianity is dying in his turn. He is dying because belief in him is dying. A classical era is finishing and a new, rigid, universal faith is advancing on the world.' This new faith was the blind subservience of the communistic, materialist, mass-produced man.

The book asserted that there were fearful pitfalls ahead of this monster. The European had already rejected feudalism (which was the attempt of the nobility to keep him poor), and fascism (which was the attempt of the middle classes to hold him back), and now an out-of-date Marxist communism and vacillating liberal democracies were contending for his soul.

Elsewhere Alex writes of a tram ride he made in Frankfurt soon after the war. The tram, he says, 'was filled with a huddle of silent, melancholy people who expected to die of cold and starvation that winter. According to medical mathematics, a good proportion of them were bound to die. They achieved an atmosphere of doom and resignation that gave the tram-ride a kind of shameful fascination; I was not going to die and they were, and there seemed something improper about our travelling together.'

He concedes that in later years the Germans made an astonishing recovery, but he did not think it was economically sound; Germany like every other country in Europe was headed for bankruptcy. In short, the new Dark Ages were to be impoverished as well as dull.

This resumé of *Enter Citizens* is not altogether fair, since there are lighter, very funny passages in the book, and it is written in an incisive and commanding style which reads just as freshly now as it did nearly two decades ago. Nor have two decades made much difference to the force of Alex's arguments. One may not agree with them but they are certainly not out of date.

I cannot remember that *Enter Citizens* made a very great stir when it first appeared. Only *The Times Literary Supplement*, I think, recognized it as something of a landmark in modern political thinking, a book that might be compared perhaps with the publication of John Strachey's *The Coming Struggle for Power* in the nineteen-thirties. Only a few thousand copies were sold and the book is hardly likely to be rediscovered and reprinted. Yet it found its target among serious people in England in 1950, and it had the effect of bringing Alex up to the threshold of that small group, the five per cent, the Establishment or whatever it is called, who rule the country.

It must have been somewhere about this time, perhaps a little earlier, that we toyed with the idea of writing a play together. It was to be a sort of pendant to *Enter Citizens*, since it dealt with the same theme, the chief difference being that it was not concerned with the fate of the mass of human beings in the modern world but with one man alone. You might have called it *Exit Citizen*. The plot was not very original. We conceived a man who is suddenly told that he has contracted an incurable disease and has only a year or two to live. What does he do? We imagined that at first he went off on a debauch, indulging all his desires while there was still time. Next he turns to religion. In the end he wishes only to go back to his job and his normal life, and death when it comes finds him doing precisely the same things he always used to do. Thus we had our three acts, and it was arranged that I should write the first draft of the dialogue which we were subsequently to polish up together.

At that time I was involved in a novel I was writing in Florence, and I put the play aside for the time being. Indeed, I almost forgot about it altogether in the welter of small happenings that always seem to overwhelm country life in Italy.

I Tatti

Florence in the nineteen-forties was the perfect balm to assuage six years of war. The tourist horde had not yet arrived, one could rent a villa for next to nothing in the hills above the town, and it was a wonderful thing after so much destruction and ugliness to live quietly in the midst of the most civilized landscape in Europe. One lunched and dined on the terrace among vines and potted flowers, the wine was good and cheap, and the books and the pictures and the ancient churches were all at hand in the town below. The war had been punctuated by arrivals and departures, but now once again it was possible to live with one's family and one's neighbours, to read, to think, to take in instead of giving out, and there were just enough visitors passing through Florence to prevent the little foreign community from becoming moribund.

The centre and focus of this capsule was Bernard Berenson and his villa I Tatti at Settignano. Now it is not for me to assess or explain Berenson; I knew him only in his old age and for a few years, most of his work was done and he was surrounded by friends and followers who were much more intimate with him than I was. Yet there was a current flowing between us, an instinctive liking; he wished me nothing but good and I knew it, he gave me all he could, and as a result he became the foster-father I so badly needed. Thus we had a mutual innocence, and although the relationship can have impinged only slightly upon him it made all the difference to me. I trusted him completely. I would not then, nor would I now, write anything or take any major decision without consciously or subconsciously summoning up the light precise voice, that detached and marvellously retentive mind, and instantly I know what I should or should not do.

Berenson clearly had his prejudices and his limitations and people no doubt will go on talking dubiously about his dealings with Duveen until the cows come home. But of all this I knew nothing; except for an occasional outburst against modern painting, most of which he loathed, he never discussed his work with me, and it also seemed to be a rule at I Tatti that one never talked about business matters or the minutiae of one's private life.

I was a queer fish in Berenson's world, and it was of course the attraction of opposites: he, the aged sophisticate who for fifty years in the most elegant surroundings had been pursuing the final subtleties and meeting the most literate people in Europe: I, the young Australian without background or connections, knowing nothing of painting or architecture, or indeed of half the subjects which were discussed so easily and in so many different languages in that elaborate and platonic house. Naturally I was in awe of him and watched my step, but even in the beginning I don't think I ever felt ill at ease with him or unable to laugh. (Though doubtless Nicky Mariano had a hand in this—presiding there at his table she could charm the embarrassment out of the most nervous guest.) And he on his side, what did he get out of me? A certain freshness perhaps, the Johnsonian pleasure of instructing a disciple, but above all, probably, affection.

We had first met some months before I came to live in Florence; he had read and liked one of my war books and through a mutual friend had invited me to stay. Then for the first time, after all the crudities, the shortage, and the do-it-yourself of the war, I had come in through the great iron gates of I Tatti and had confronted the butler, and had seen my dusty luggage borne away through corridors of paintings, and, tense as a cat among the dishes and the Venetian fingerbowls, had kept afloat through dinner, and had then woken in the morning to observe the valet who, thermometer in hand, had come to run my bath, and who had brought my breakfast tray with its little posy of flowers and copies of *Il Corriere della Sera*, the *Zuricher Zeitung* and the London *Times*, only two days old. Then too I had had my initiatory walk down the avenue of ilexes to the reflecting pool, and through the wild ground to the hedges of the lower formal garden and back to the orangery for tea, Berenson chatting all the way and the guests trailing behind him as polite, as self-conscious and as gracious as the figures in a Japanese print.

This, I say, was the initiation, and now that I had come to live at San Domenico da Fiesole, Berenson and his library and his talk lay just over the other side of the hill. And so our friendship had time to develop; we met for two years with fair regularity and later on sporadically (when I was living elsewhere) until his death. I kept a diary during the Florence period, and on opening it now, twenty years later, I am astonished and embarrassed to find how false one's memory can be. Things that I emphasized then have long vanished from my mind, stories that I have since repeated about Berenson are revealed by the diary to have been if not inaccurate then at least a re-arrangement of the truth; and the golden glow with which I see those years in retrospect was not quite so golden at the time. The slow process of editing that presumably goes on in everybody's mind, the rejection of some things in the past and the summoning up of others, the desire for coherence and a pattern, the unconscious but deliberate muddling of dates—all this is coldly exposed by my diary, and it makes one wonder if anything *but* diaries can be accurate, at any rate upon points of fact. I do not even appear to have been much impressed by Berenson at the beginning. Early in the diary there is a tart note: 'When the old man says, "So you believe that the mass of the people can be educated," and laughs; when he says,

"Universal suffrage is rubbish. Why then not give domestic animals the vote? Only those who have political education should vote," I find I have nothing to bring against such Edwardian quaintness. It's not worth answering.'

Berenson talked a great deal about politics in those days, and among his *obiter dicta* I remember him saying that no people ever feel secure until they have succeeded in persecuting somebody else; thus in America the Spaniards demolished the Incas and the Puritans the Red Indians, and so it would go with the state of Israel which was just then coming into being; the Israelis were bound to assert themselves against the Arabs until they could stand on their own feet. But the great aim of politics should always be, he thought, to establish a balance of power. Whenever that balance was lost war and anarchy supervened.

For myself I wanted to know nothing of these things, for the time being I had had enough of wars and politics. I wanted to drink my wine, to talk of the past and to be free to spend long silent hours in the library at I Tatti. I read Symonds' volumes on the Italian renaissance, and then went on to make a study of Angelo Poliziano, the poet and friend of Lorenzo the Magnificent. It was Poliziano's old house, built at San Domenico da Fiesole four hundred years before, that I had rented.

Berenson was amused at this. 'Why are you bothering about him?' he asked.

'Because he fascinates me.'

'Well, he fascinates me too. He was an interesting chap but with no real intellect. You might dip him into what I call the sauce of the epoch, but then the little shrimp would disappear.'

He was obsessed by the English—probably because in his heart he quite wanted to be an Englishman himself. There was a good deal about his appearance that reminded one of King George V of England. He was older and more

fragile than King George ever became, but his beautifully
trimmed beard had the royal air, there was almost a
nautical jauntiness in his spruce and alert little figure, and
although he was such a tiny man one never thought him so.
As for his voice, it was as precise and as beautifully
modulated as the phrases he uttered, and it contained no
trace of an American accent that I could discover. He
appeared to be equally exact in French and Italian and
several other languages as well.

Sometimes in the winter in arriving at I Tatti I would
find him in the garden, and he would be wearing white
gloves, trouser cuffs neatly turned up against the mud, a
felt hat on his head and a shawl round his shoulders. He
was always immaculate and perhaps in the end, next to
affection, it was precision that he valued as much as anything else in life. Precisely at 1 p.m., when we were all
assembled for lunch, he would appear, deft and courteous,
and shepherd us into the dining room. He ate very little,
drank hardly at all, and never smoked (I am speaking of
him when he was in his eighties), and when the meal was
over he would remain with his guests for exactly half an
hour, when he would go off for his rest, only to bob up
again, as regular as clockwork, for tea and a walk in the
garden.

In the mornings he wrote his letters and worked in bed.
In the evening Nicky would read to him from one of
several books that happened to interest him at the
moment. His memory was quite phenomenal; he could
quote stories that Oscar Wilde had told at a London
dinner table half a century before, and apparently there was
no book of any merit that he had not read. Once when I
had been asked by an American publisher to write a life of
Benevenuto Cellini I went to him for advice, and he said:
'No, you must not do it. There is nothing new to be had
except an essay of Goethe's which has not yet been translated into English and it's not very interesting. You

could, of course, make a study of Florence in Cellini's time, but it would take you many years and you are not, I think, quite scholar enough for that.' He paused and went on: 'But what a wonderful book Cellini's is. Do you remember that passage . . .' and he quoted verbatim a page or two from the original Italian version which he had last read, he said—and I believed him—twenty-five years before.

He did not often speak of himself, but he told me once that as a young man he had gone across to Toledo in Spain to see the El Grecos and had then taken the train back to Barcelona. This train stopped for an hour or two at Madrid —just long enough for him to walk to the Prado, make a quick tour of the galleries, and get back to the station on time. On the way down to Barcelona he found that he remembered every one of the thousand paintings he had seen.

This strength of mind was chained to a physical fragility that was quite frightening at times. It was not that his sight or hearing failed—they remained unusually good almost to the very end—but those delicate blue-veined hands had the translucency of porcelain, he was as thin as a ghost and altogether too light and buoyant; one puff of wind, it seemed, might blow him away. And indeed after I had left Florence he had a fearful accident. He was standing on top of an embankment admiring a view when a buffet of wind slammed the car door upon him and he lost his footing. Down the embankment he went, rolling over and over like a piece of thistledown until at last he came to rest inert and unconscious at the bottom. And yet he lived. There was something in his very fragility that preserved him. In the upheaval of the war and its aftermath most of his contemporaries died, but like the one piece of brittle china that miraculously escapes the blast in a bombed house he continued to live on.

Berenson, for all his authority, was rather exposed because he ranged so widely and speculated so much. Then too he could not be alone, he liked to have people about him and an audience. There was a tremendous flow of visitors through I Tatti in these post-war years, and it increased as time went on; a lunch party, a tea-party and a dinner-party almost every day, and nearly always two or three house guests. It would be ridiculous to suggest that Berenson surrounded himself with sycophants; still, there was a penumbra of adulation about the house, an atmosphere of the court, and it irritated some people.

Nor would it have been difficult to criticize the house itself. Much of the furniture was lumpish and even ugly, and the rooms were too small and dark. There were of course beautiful objects in every corner, but perhaps there were too many of them for a house that was not yet a museum. I remember one night being there alone—the family had gone up to the hills at Vallambrosa and the servants were in their own rooms at the rear—and I inadvertently switched out all the lights. By no amount of groping on the wall could I find the switches again and so there was nothing for it but to make my way to the front door some fifty yards away in total darkness. Ornaments and glass shelves filled with breakable *objets d'art* lay, I knew, on every side, and after the first few steps I lost my nerve. I dropped to my hands and knees and inch by inch edged my way along the corridors, every instant portending some terrible crash, until at last like a cat-burglar I found the door and escaped into the night.

The library was much the best part of the house, and year by year it grew until it occupied a dozen rooms or more, all of them beautifully furnished and arranged. The books were mainly upon art and architecture, but there was an extensive general library as well, and so I used often to come over to I Tatti and work there through the morning. My work was not going particularly well, and looking back now I see I ought to have done more reading and less writing at the time. I finished a novel but it read badly and I put it away in a drawer with a feeling of failure and despair.

*

To make a break we went up to stay for a few days with Ernest Hemingway and his fourth wife, Mary, who happened to be an old friend of ours; they had taken a chalet at Cortina in the Italian Dolomites. We arrived in heavy snow, and Hemingway was out shooting duck, a gruelling business in that weather since it involved standing by the hour in a barrel in a frozen marsh waiting for the dawn to break. When he came in at last he was the walking myth of himself. Cartridge belts and strings of teal and mallard hung in festoons from his shoulders, powdered snow clung to his beard and woolly cap, and when his gun was laid aside in the corner he had to be helped off with his clothes—layer after layer of sweaters, leather jerkins and a coloured shirt. At the end of it all he fished a cable out of his pocket and held it out to me. It read: 'Nothing could be better than a piece on Venice by you but it so happens we have got someone called Alan Moorehead who may be doing it one day so I am sorry . . .' It was signed Harold Ross.

This was both embarrassing and ridiculous, and it also helps to explain why Harold Ross was more loved than any other editor of his time. Two years before in New York he had suggested to me over lunch that I should write for the *New Yorker* an article on Venice, and I had demurred, saying that I disliked Venice, that the place gave me claustrophobia, that unpleasant things always happened to me when I went there, I got a cold, I lost my passport, I had rows with my friends. Ross answered simply, 'Oh well, one day you may do it.' That was all that passed between us, there was nothing more. And now after two years Hemingway, the most sought-after writer

of his generation, had cabled Ross saying he had been in
Venice for a month and would like to write an article about
it, and had had this reply.

Hemingway was not very welcoming. 'When I heard at
first you were coming,' he said, 'I thought I'd move out so
as to give you a bit more room around the place with
Mary.' When he said this I imagined that, incredibly, he
had taken offence over Ross's cable, and it was only later
on that I realized that he regarded us as Mary's friends,
and as such we were an intrusion into his private life. He
liked to have his own friends in the house, and he liked to
absorb them entirely. More, he too was miserable. He was
in the midst of one of those dreadful depressions in a
writer's life when nothing flows, nothing comes, the words
lie dead, banal and empty in the head. He filled in the
writing hours of the day by typing interminable letters.
He was not even ski-ing, and when I wanted to take Mary
out he was against it. 'She can't ski. She'll break her leg.'

'I'll look after her.'

In the end he gave in, and Mary, my wife and I set off in
bright sunshine for the ski-lift. It was not a good day,
however, the snow was frozen in some places and soft and
wet in others. Mary made a run into one of these soft
patches, fell down and did not get up.

'Come on,' I said.

'I can't. I've broken my leg.'

It was a long time before we found a sleigh in one of
the farms nearby and got her down to the hospital in the
village, and it was well after two o'clock when I telephoned
Hemingway at the chalet. He was furious. For two hours
or more he had been sitting there awaiting and dreading
this message, and now he let go with four-letter words.
His temper improved somewhat when we got back with
Mary from the hospital, but still my wife and I would have
left at once had not poor Mary, confined to her bedroom
upstairs, been in need of her company. This left me

downstairs with Hemingway, and there we sat and talked for the next three or four days.

I do not know how he talked to other people, but to me he always talked of books, always of writing, and with the humility and doubt of a writer who reads for five hours or so every day, and who writes and re-writes for as long as his brain will work, knowing that it is only by a miracle that he will ever achieve a phrase, even a word, that will correspond to the vision in his mind.

The truncated joke-language of Hemingway's talk—the dropping of the definite article, the vulgar phrase to describe the solemn thing—for which he was so well known and so often quoted, vanished; or if it did not vanish one ceased to notice it because he was a very serious man when he was not putting up a façade. He had the art of cursing without malice, he talked of sex without being dirty, and his enthusiasms were genuine enthusiasms; when all was said and done he liked to hunt, he preferred the company of bullfighters and boxers to his contemporaries, and if the world came to think of him as a bully-boy with a flair for publicity and a secret fear of lapsing in his virility, it did not know him. He was a violent, quick-tempered man and an egotist, he could behave meanly and outrageously in his private life, but he was not frightened, he was certainly not a bore, and publicity sought him out, not he it; for thirty years or more he buried himself away in the country, refusing ever to lecture or to appear on television or indeed make any public appearance of any kind whatever. He would not even go to Stockholm to receive the Nobel prize. No film company ever lured him to Hollywood to act or write. No party could get him to enter politics. No hostess had a hope in heaven of parading him in society. No one ever got him to deviate from his work. And with his work he was a lonely man.

And so now, sitting at a wooden table in the chalet, with

a fiasco of red wine between us and the snow outside, we talked about writing. He had begun his education, he said, as a reporter in the police courts by listening carefully to the confused and stumbling evidence given by witnesses. At home at night he would re-write this evidence as clearly and simply as possible, but always using the words the witness would have used. Then he would take this précis and infuse into it his own interpretation of the witness and of what he had to say, but still only using those words which the witness would have naturally used, and which would be intelligible to anyone who had not been in the court. Then again he would reduce and simplify this material until, by repeated processes of synthesis and distillation he arrived at what he believed to be the true essence of the evidence. 'The only contribution I've made,' he said, 'has been to clarify the language.' He wrote, he said, forty different endings to *A Farewell to Arms*, and they were all variations of the same theme.

Speaking of writing fiction, he said that he never knew what was going to follow from one page to the next; one was simply seized with an idea, and if the writer truly expressed his feelings the plot and eventually the style and pattern of the book would take care of themselves. Thus one day in Paris he saw a man and a woman sitting together upstairs in Prunier's restaurant, and he instantly knew that she had just had an abortion—a scene something like Manet's *L'absinthe*, one imagines. And he thought of himself and his own wife in that situation, not in Prunier's but in a railway station in Spain he happened to know about. Why in Spain? No reason. He called the story *Hills like White Elephants*.

The rewards of his past work were, of course, very great. Yet another anthology of his writings had just come out, *The Portable Hemingway* ('All that's potable,' he said), and *A Farewell to Arms* had sold 300,000 copies in Denmark *since* the war—'surely saturation point'.

Hemingway at that time was still very robust, and not drinking much except red wine. One night in the piazza at Cortina an Alsatian and another big dog began to fight in the snow, surrounded by screaming women, and Hemingway, throwing his coat over the Alsatian, picked it up in his arms and threw it bodily over the wall, a masterful bit of business in his true *genre*. Yet there was a certain gloom overhanging the chalet—the gloom of his not being able to work I think—and we were a little sad about them as we came away.

*

In Florence I sat down again to try and force myself to write. I remember so well the rooms where I have written books, these cells, these self-inflicted prisons where the writer sits incarcerated for so many hours each day—so many words a day, so many chapters in a month. With the beginning of each new book he isolates himself from contemporary life; like a tree in winter he ceases to make an outward show but instead drives his roots downward into the past where he hopes to find, in the store of his experiences, the food for his inspiration.

And so a writer's books are the chapters of his life and the rooms where he writes them are the real setting of his existence. Although he may have been oblivious at the time of the surrounding walls, of the chair and the table and of the view through the window, he will remember these things afterwards with unusual clarity because he associates them with a particular book and with all the circumstances of its creation.

In my own case I remember very well the flat on the island in the Nile in Cairo, where I wrote my first book; during the war a cabin on a French ship carrying German prisoners on a long voyage half way round the world to Canada; and a farm in Kent. Then after the war there was a shed at the bottom of a lemon grove in Australia, a

terrace at Portofino, and now this villa in Florence, the
dark room with the two high windows and a long re-
fectory table.

And still I was reduced to a state of helpless and
frustrating idleness, casting about for something to get
my teeth into. The fact was that my breakaway from daily
journalism and its safe factual routine was proving altogether too tough. I had half a dozen books behind me now,
but these were mostly about the war, and I had not yet
learned how to work from within myself; but for Berenson
I might have lost heart altogether. He himself wrote with
great difficulty and never really achieved a satisfactory
style; writing was too slow for him, his brain teemed with
ideas, speculations and shades of meaning, and he was
forever cramming too much into a sentence, forever trying
to make words fly as fast as conversation. Nevertheless he
kept doggedly at it, believing that clarity and inspiration
would arrive at last, and he advised me to do the same
thing.

I would have liked to have written Berenson's own life,
but he rejected this: 'No, I want nothing written and no
publicity while I am alive.' He really did hate public
appearances and refused to make a speech when the
Italians presented him with two gold medals in the
Palazzo Strozzi in Florence in 1948. 'There he sat,' wrote
the correspondent of the *Corriere della Sera*, 'dumb,
monolithic and probably deaf.' This pleased Berenson very
much.

Presently I began to suffer from that dreadful ennui that
must overtake all self-appointed exiles who live in beautiful places in the sun. One lovely day succeeded another,
the outlook was always upon cypresses and flowers and
olive groves, every village church and contadino's cottage
was part of the even texture of the landscape and nothing
was vile. One lived like a queen bee, cossetted and
cherished, and all the world was honey. Had one been born

and brought up in Florence things might have been different; then one would have had a share of responsibility for what was going on around one, and associations reaching back into the past. But as things were it mattered not in the least to me who won the local elections or whether the hail destroyed the grapes or whether or not Florence defeated Turin at football.

The manifest correction for this detachment was work, but it was not always possible to work, and by the end of the second year the usual distractions began to fall into a wearisome routine. One made a patience of living. Meeting the same people all the time conversation declined into gossip, and good food became monotonous, and having seen the pictures in the Uffizi and the sunset light from San Miniato for the twentieth time one did not want to go to those places any more. Even the enthusiasm of one's friends arriving from the bleak and ugly north was not enough to break up this log-jam of satiety, this sickly vacuity, this creeping paralysis in the soft air. 'Another bad day,' runs an entry in my diary, 'with ennui only just held at bay by manufacturing a round of minor things to do. Time, Machiavelli says, drives everything before it. Not me.'

Berenson himself, I fancy, also feared this emptiness; that is why he forced himself to work every day, that is why he surrounded himself with so many people. But he was eighty and I was forty and his work really did lie here, he had his roots. Fifty years or more ago, as a penniless young man he had gone over the frescoes in these Tuscan churches inch by inch, riding out each morning on his bicycle with his pocket full of candles to light the dusky corners, returning at night to write up his notes—and home then was a pensione on the Arno. He had visited every church in Tuscany, he had written his books, he had built his villa, he had his library, his friends, his fame and his disciples; Florence was where he had to be. But for me it did not really matter whether I was in Florence or not, I was perching here in a rented villa making a mental convalescence from the war, and there were times when, in an extremity of boredom, deserts of nothingness on every side, I would go over to I Tatti just to clutch my way back to life again, the faithful hound in search of his master's voice.

He could not really help beyond a certain point. Help lay over the horizon in a noisier, less improving place than this. He could and did help me in a way a psychiatrist can by putting a name to my tedium and by analysing my plight. But finally there was nothing to analyse any more, all had been explained, my cure was making me ill.

When it was decided I was to go, Florence never looked more beautiful or more safe and secure. The nostalgia set in even before I packed my bags—nostalgia for the conversation with Berenson now broken, for Poliziano's villa and the people who had worked for me there, for the garden we had planted, for the many friends we had made amongst the other denizens of the capsule. And later from London, from Paris, from New York and other crowded places, even from Greece, Tuscany still glowed like some childhood memory of a summer holiday.

To the Edgware Road   V

JUST BEFORE I left Florence a letter arrived from Alex in Germany saying that a lump the size of a tennis ball had appeared under his arm. 'They say', he wrote, 'that I have an incurable disease and I have to go back to London to see about it.'

He wrote, as usual, in his clear round handwriting, with the same familiar wide spacing between the lines, the same detached dry style, and it seemed madness that this letter should be saying what it said, that it should be so enormously, hideously different from the scores of others we had received from him. We reassured ourselves: how could the German doctor possibly know for certain? Tremendous advances had been made in medicine during the war, there was now *some* answer to every disease; penicillin, the new anti-biotics. We would hear a very different story from the London specialists.

Alex was already in England when we arrived there. He looked the same, he walked about as usual, ate the same food, talked in the same way, and he said: 'It's a thing called Hodgkin's Disease. You have two years to live.'

'Is that definite?'

'No, nothing is definite. They are experimenting all the time.'

'But what *is* it?'

'Nobody knows. I suppose it's a sort of cancer.'

'Are they giving you any treatment?'

'Oh yes, I'm having a series of deep X-rays in the hospital and when it's finished I can go off and do whatever I want. But I will have to come back in a few months for another treatment.'

He had been ill before. I had left him once, huddled up with sandfly fever, on his camp bed in the desert. He had been in hospital for a few days in Brussels with some sort of trouble in his ear. He had had the bout of jaundice at the time of the D-day landing. But he had recovered from all these. Why should there be this blank finality about the doctors' diagnosis this time? How could they be so certain? How could anyone be struck down like this out of the blue? Alex never smoked, scarcely drank, lived the most healthy of lives. Why pick on him?

He had gone to our own family doctor, a friend we had known for years, and when Lucy and I went to see this doctor he was not reassuring. He merely repeated what Alex had said. The X-ray treatment would serve for a time but later its effects would grow less and less. Outwardly Alex would appear quite normal, but in reality he would be dying. And in pain? Yes, at times in pain, but there were drugs. At the end there was a treatment with mustard gas, but it could only delay death for a short time. Sometimes for unknown reasons a patient would linger on for quite long periods, but as a rule death followed two years after the first symptoms appeared. Was there no hope that some new remedy would be discovered? Yes, it was a high-priority subject for research at the Johns Hopkins University in the United States, but as yet they had hit upon nothing new. Were there not other, better, specialists than the ones in London whom Alex should see? No, all the present knowledge of the disease and the means of treating it were available here. Was he sure about this? Yes, he was sure.

I cannot pretend to know much about the days that followed, but one had a glimpse of what was going on from occasional things that Alex let drop. When he called at the hospital for treatment one day he found that a woman patient who was also suffering from Hodgkin's Disease had thrown herself down the lift-shaft rather than

face the ordeal of the X-rays. Alex went on to his appoint-
ment. I thought that I myself must have gone mad in these
circumstances, but Alex did not go mad. He remained
very sane. When he was released from his hospital
appointments he travelled down to Portofino with Jenny.

He did not, like the man in our play, indulge in a
debauch, and I don't think he ever contemplated it. Instead he remained quietly at Portofino, writing a little,
helping Jenny in the many things they were always doing
to improve their villa. Then, equally unobtrusively, he
moved on to Act Two; he went down to Rome, there to
explore with two Monsignori he knew the means by
which a man can embrace the Roman Catholic faith. When
I asked him about this afterwards he said shortly, 'It
didn't work.' That was all. We never really discussed the
matter again and in any case this phase was soon followed
by Act Three: more and more Alex found that it was his
one desire to go on with his work as a foreign correspondent. Most of the time he was fit enough to travel and
travel he did, writing his articles as before, not so many of
them, and they were not quite so trenchant, but still they
contained that admirable accuracy of fact, followed by the
unexpected, devastating deduction.

He would have preferred to spend more time at
Portofino, for he was forming now a really deep attach-
ment to the place, but that was not possible, partly because
he was determined to go on with his work and partly
because he was bound to return to London from
time to time for further treatment. Moreover the only
approach to the Castelletto was by a steep fifteen-minute
climb on foot from the village, and it was clear that he
would not be able to manage this indefinitely. He grew a
little thinner in the face but otherwise he did not change
greatly. Never at any stage now or later did he lose hope,
and never in my presence did he give way to despair or
even complaint. It was all so outwardly normal, so slow,

so uneventful, that we began to think, as the months went
by and the first of these deadly years passed into the
second, that it was all a kind of nightmare from which
presently Alex would wake up. One cannot contemplate
the inevitability of early death—he was still only forty-
two—unless there are deep and evident ravages beforehand. But then unlike Jenny we were not much with Alex
through these days; we only saw him when he came to
London where we had moved from Florence soon after his
treatment began. None of his letters revealed the terrible
crises in the night, the sweatings, the stricken breathless-
ness. He and Jenny had taken a flat in Albany, and we used
to dine there or at our own house off Regents Park, and
sometimes go on together to a cinema or a theatre. For a
while in the summer of 1951 it really did begin to look as
though the disease, if not diminishing, was at least
stationary, but then one day we heard that he had gone
back to hospital.

It was by now generally known by Alex's friends that he
was facing calamity, and strange people would appear,
acquaintances of whom I had never heard, to offer their
help. A millionaire he scarcely knew wanted to fly him by
private plane to the Johns Hopkins University, to China,
anywhere. Others whom he could only have known
casually, doorkeepers of hotels, minor officials, travellers
met by chance on a voyage, wrote most moving letters.
The five per cent was stirred and inquiries came from
cabinet ministers, actresses, dons and churchmen, both
Protestant and Catholic. I think they were moved even
more by Alex himself than by his plight; he was a rare
bird and they felt they could not let him die.

By the winter of 1951 the prescribed time was growing
very short, but I do not think Alex concerned himself too
much with this. Always the implication was: this is a
special case. It won't go the usual way. Something will
turn up. He was still up and about and one day we hit on a

plan that delighted us all; we would have a fortnight's ski-ing in Austria. Ski-ing had once been his passion, and now, in the midst of this dreary London winter, it offered a marvellous escape into fresh air and sunshine. Alex had been receiving treatment in hospital once again, and it was arranged that he should first go down to Italy to re-cuperate, and that he and Jenny should make a rendezvous with Lucy and myself at the White Horse Inn in Kitzbühl in January. He wrote to us from Portofino saying that he was getting on well enough, but that he had found the walk up to the Castelletto too much and consequently was staying in a flat in the village below. He was in Rome with Jenny for Christmas, and once again he wrote cheerfully, though he admitted he was having difficulty in sleeping at night. Towards the middle of January Lucy and I set out by train from London for Kitzbühl, and Alex and Jenny came north from Rome.

It was a hard winter. Lines of icicles formed along the eaves of the hotel, and there was not enough warmth in the short cloudy days to melt them. But the hotel was cheer-ful and lively and there was blinding sunshine on the heights above. We soon developed a routine: a picnic lunch in the sun at one or other of the little chalets at the tops of the ski-runs, the run down through the middle of the day, tea with chocolate cakes in the village, then the blessed all-embracing hot bath, martinis, dinner and canasta. Alex kept it up for a few days and then had a bad night. Jenny was up more than once changing his pyjamas and sheets as they became wringing wet. There was very little the local doctor could do except try and drug the pain, and Alex was forced to potter around the hotel or lie in bed. Sometimes he roused himself to go out, but it was not for long.

Curiously I cannot remember any atmosphere of alarm or gloom about these days. We talked, often we laughed, as we had always done, we had a number of friends about us, and Alex came down to meals like any other guest. One night we all went off in a sleigh to a fancy dress ball in the town, and it seemed that his strength was returning. He proposed that he and I on the following morning should go up to the highest run of all and thence ski down eight miles to a neighbouring valley where we would find a local train to bring us home again.

It was a raw morning, next day, and even when we reached the heights the sun had not really broken through. Being one of the worst of ski-ers I baulked a little at the ice and the steepness of the descent. But Alex, wrapped in a black jacket, his head in a bright woollen cap, spread his wings and flew. He skimmed away into the milky space like some great black bird on the wing, and when I re-joined him after several headlong falls at the bottom of the first run he was grinning. I was breathless and dis-hevelled.

'Can't you take it a little slower?'

'No. Come on.'

Then he was off again, gliding and swooping down the mountain, and I, gaining confidence, launched myself in pursuit. I caught him up presently, and now, when a little sunshine had broken through, we raced on together across enormous slopes. It was a wonderful thing: the sun shin-ing, the crunch of the snow under the skis, and we two, moving in unison very fast with the wind rushing by. It really was like flying. On the lower slopes we began to catch up with other parties, and here on broken ground and in softer snow the going was heavy. At times we had to walk through slush and pick our way through protrud-ing roots and rocks. A plump Italian woman, clearly a novice and a desperate one at that, vanished headfirst into an unexpected drift, and we pulled her out of it. Her face, as she surfaced, expressed the extreme of human woe.

'E tremenda!' was all she could say. 'Mamma mia, e tremenda!'

And it was in fact very tiring. When we got down to the road in the valley we took off our skis and tramped heavily along to the station, half a mile away. We bought tickets to Kitzbühl and sat in the steamy little waiting room drinking hot wine laced with cinnamon. When the train came in a crowd of healthy young Austrians clattered on board with their skis, but we found seats on opposite wooden benches. I looked across at Alex and saw that his face had gone a ghastly shade of whitish green. There was a little foam on his lip and he sat there absolutely still, looking out of the window but obviously seeing nothing, since his eyes were glazed and dull. So we sat for half an hour with the lively voices and the laughter of the young Austrians all about us, and when this eternity had gone by we found a sled at Kitzbühl station and rode in silence back to the hotel. That night he had a relapse. He could not sleep. He could not rest. The pain increased. After two days and nights of this we got on the train and went back to London.

When we arrived he did not want us to come in with him to Albany and so we went home and telephoned the doctor. That night he was moved into hospital.

The next six weeks were a strange period of suspended time, a twilight that seemed to be going on forever. Alex had passed the two-year mark and the X-ray treatment was no longer effective. He was too weak for it anyway. Increasingly now he had to be drugged to keep the pain at bay, and although he was often listless when we went to see him there remained about him that same strange air of normality, of a crisis that was somehow not a crisis. More than once we went to the doctors and said, surely this cannot be the end: how can you say so when he seems so normal? But they were adamant. The most they would say was that, just possibly, after this bout he could go back to Albany, perhaps even to Portofino.

Alex himself seemed, if anything, more than ever

convinced that he would recover. Now the letters and visits from relatives and friends redoubled, and the room blossomed with flowers out of season and tropical fruit. A Catholic friend arrived with a priest and a sacred relic to conduct a service. Specialists came and nurses appeared with new drugs and injections. Alex took the liveliest interest in all this, debating his treatment with the doctors, debating religion with priests, listening attentively when we told him stories of the outside world. Then one day he seemed to lose interest. He did not want to argue or listen any more. The listlessness now was a true listlessness, the crisis was real at last. When we went to see him he was sometimes too lost in his own world of drugs and pain to notice we were there. Jenny, Lucy and myself took turns to sit with him.

Now only the mustard gas treatment remained. It seemed to us three, as we watched Alex sinking, that there was no point in going on with this life, this aimless drawn-out ordeal which could only protract existence a few more days, at the most a few weeks. The end was always going to be the same. We must have all come to this dreadful conclusion about the same time, because I remember that we stood in the corridor outside Alex's room and quite spontaneously we brought our thoughts out into the open: Alex had made his fight. Now he must be allowed to die. When the specialist in charge arrived we broached the matter directly. His reply was short and harsh: 'No one,' he said, 'dies in this hospital so long as he has the slightest chance of living, even for a few more hours.'

That night Alex was given the mustard gas treatment. When it was my turn to go and sit with him on the following day I was surprised to see a great change in him. His eyes were open and there was a bright feverish light in them. For several days past he had not spoken to me or shown any really definite sign that he knew me. Now he half turned his head towards me and began to speak.

'You were quite wrong yesterday,' he said slowly. 'They were absolutely right to give me the mustard gas. It's wonderful.'

What could one say? Could I protest that he could not possibly have known what I said to the specialist? He knew.

'Yes,' he went on. 'It's wonderful.'

There was a long pause, and it was evident that he was struggling to say something more, something which was of great importance to him.

When he began again his voice was very low and disjointed but full of excitement. 'I see it all now. There are two sides, two levels. On one level I am vulgar . . . disgusting . . .' (I think the word was disgusting). 'But on the other level . . . clear . . . beautiful . . .'

It was a vision of some kind and his voice went rambling on, faint and meaningless and I could understand no more. But this hardly mattered. What was important was that I had been wrong about the mustard gas, for it had obviously conjured up in his mind an ecstasy which had filled him with an inexpressible joy. And this after so many months of agony, so many years of doubt and hesitation. Now at last he seemed to feel that all was explained.

I sat there calling to him, straining to listen, bending my head down to his lips. He was now quite silent but I could see by his eyes that he recognized me. It was thus that the sister found us a little later, and she had hardly come into the room when Alex began to struggle for breath and there was a dry rattle in his throat, a terrible thing to hear. The pupils of his eyes turned upwards and the whites began to show beneath. The nurse ran from the room, and presently the wheels of a trolley sounded in the corridor. Two or three nurses came in with an oxygen respirator and fixed it to Alex's mouth. He responded very slowly and we watched in silence.

I got up hurriedly then, intending to find a telephone, but I had advanced only a few steps down the corridor when I realized I had no means of finding Jenny and Lucy. They had gone out to lunch saying they would relieve me in an hour, but they had not said where they were going. They might have been in any of twenty different restaurants. I went back into the room. The struggle now was going with great difficulty and the awful rattle seemed to gain with every feeble breath. Quite visibly the grey paralysis of death was creeping over Alex's face.

'If you want to say anything to him,' one of the nurses said, 'say it now.'

Where were the others? Ought they not too be saying something? What was there for me to say except that I loved him? I said this but there was no answer. I called to him again. The nurses stood round listening. When Jenny and Lucy came in his breathing was barely perceptible and presently it stopped altogether.

They are wonderfully efficient in a modern hospital. There was a quick adroit scurry of nurses about the body and within a few seconds we were ushered out of the room. We stood together in the corridor waiting for something— we did not know what. There did not seem to be any particular place to which we ought to go. Presently however I was led downstairs to a sort of ante-room near the entrance of the hospital, and I found a small neat man in a dark suit waiting for me there. He too was marvellously soothing and efficient.

'I understand you are in charge of the arrangements?'

Yes, I supposed I was.

'Then if you will leave the matter in our hands. There are just a few little details to decide.'

It was wonderfully done. We agreed upon the type of coffin, the kind of wood, the handles, the question of cars, the flowers. There was nothing for me to sign, nothing to bother about; all could be left to this polite and tactful

man. I had, however, one more question to ask. What was
to happen to Alex now—tonight?

'We will take care of the remains and keep them on our
premises until the hour of the service.'

'And where is your . . .' What should one say? Place
of business? Funeral parlour? I compromised on 'place'.

Swift as a thrush he plucked a visiting card from his
pocket and I read the address. It was in the Edgware Road.